The Chinese Sharing Economy

Ma Huateng · Zhang Xiaorong · Sun Yi ·
Cai Xiongshan

The Chinese Sharing Economy

New Economy Program for Supply-Side Reform

Produced by: Tencent Research Institute

palgrave
macmillan

Ma Huateng
Tencent Research Institute
Shenzhen, China

Zhang Xiaorong
Tencent Research Institute
Shenzhen, China

Sun Yi
Tencent Research Institute
Shenzhen, China

Cai Xiongshan
Tencent Research Institute
Shenzhen, China

Editors-in-Chief
Guo Kaitian
Shenzhen, China

Si Xiao
Shenzhen, China

ISBN 978-981-33-6496-7 ISBN 978-981-33-6494-3 (eBook)
https://doi.org/10.1007/978-981-33-6494-3

Jointly published with CITIC Press Corporation
The print edition is not for sale in China Mainland. Customers from China Mainland please order the print book from: CITIC Press Corporation.
ISBN of the Co-Publisher's edition: 9787508661049

Translated from the Chinese language edition: **分享经济：供给侧改革的新经济方案**,

This Palgrave Macmillan imprint is published by the registered company Springer Nature Singapore Pte Ltd.
The registered company address is: 152 Beach Road, #21-01/04 Gateway East, Singapore 189721, Singapore

Team of Creators
Ma Huateng
Zhang Xiaorong, Sun Yi, and Cai Xiongshan

Publishers
Guo Kaitian and Si Xiao

Special Consultants
Cheng Wei, Brent Irvin, Xie Hu, and Jiang Yang

Foreword by Cheng Wei: Vision of a Practitioner Amid the Surging Sharing Economy

The solicitation for a foreword for this book with me exactly coincided with the closing of the 2016 CPPCC and NPC sessions, where Chinese Premier Li Keqiang touched on the topic of sharing economy twice in his *Report on the Work of the Government*: "promoting the development of sharing economy" and "supporting the development of sharing economy". The evolution of the expression about sharing economy from "developing sharing economy" in the previous literature of China's Central Government to "promoting the development of sharing economy" and "supporting the development of sharing economy" obviously highlighted an increasing role of sharing economy in China's overall economic landscape. With distinct features, including popular participation, more efficient resource allocation and better user experience, the new economic mode of "access over ownership" in sharing economy not only dovetails with the requirements of the supply-side structural reform but also meets the potential consumer demand, and thus has rapidly risen to lend fresh impetus to the further economic development in China. We are very pleased to see that Didi has risen to be a brave standard-bearer and unflagging practitioner in the booming sharing economy.

Three years or so ago, we succeeded in connecting taxis and passengers through information matching. Later, we found out that taxi service remained unavailable to numerous passengers during rush hours even if a staggering 80% proportion of the taxi drivers signed in for the Didi platform, so we launched more options: tailored taxi service and fast ride service.

But soon afterward, we found that no matter how many full-time taxi drivers are ready to offer service on the platform, the demand couldn't be completely satisfied during peak periods, so we combined B2C with C2C to leverage the spare time and idle resources of part-time drivers. With the sharing economy model of "let everyone help others", it would be possible for us to solve perfectly the issue of the unbalance between supply and demand in different periods a day. With this in mind, we rolled out in a quick sequence a series of new services: fast ride service, fast carpooling, Didi hitch, inter-city Didi Hitch.

So far, we have successfully solved the issue of insufficient access to taxi services by raising the response rate and the rate of successful deal-matching in taxi-hailing to more than 90% and 60% respectively, and introduced and promoted the model and concept of sharing economy in more than 400 cities across the country, having the convenience and comfort brought about by sharing economy really felt by more than 250 million Chinese citizens.

Didi's dream in travel is to have all vehicles be connected to the Internet so as to marshal all the vehicles on road and navigate traffic flows on road via increasingly powerful cloud-based traffic applications and increasingly intelligent search engines to improve the overall travel efficiency in urban regions and deliver better travel experience of all travelers. As the sharing economy mode gains traction, there will no longer any need of putting additional private cars on the road in every Chinese city. Our mission remains the same: Having a More Relaxing Journey, and our aspiration also remains unchanged: to be the largest one-stop travel platform in the world.

The rapid development of Didi over the past half-year prompted me to ponder over these questions: why did sharing economy boom overnight in the internet age? Why did it get so popular first in the travel sector? Why has Didi emerged the poster boy of sharing economy? How promising is the prospect for sharing economy in China? Now, I would like to give my answers to these questions in the following four dimensions:

First, resource constraints in the late industrial age are the context for the rise of sharing economy.

In the industrial age, the privatization of real right led to the concept of ownership. With the mass industrial production and the resulting extremely abundant supply of commodities, ownership economy had grown at neck-breaking paces until the late industrial age, namely somewhere in the recent decade or so, when resource shortages began to loom larger over time in various sectors. The world came aware that it is unfeasible for everyone to own as much as he wishes, as there are limits too many things, including air, transportation resources, energy sources, and many others. Limited resources can't sustain everyone's desire for unlimited ownership. This is just the first macro background.

Second, the most pioneering sharing economy emerged first in those most resource-starved sectors.

The lack of transportation resources or road resources is the primary bottleneck to constrain the development of the transportation sector in China. Over the past decade or so, road development has failed to keep pace with the exploding car population. Are there, really, too many cars in China? The answer is a sounding answer: "No, not at all". In fact, there are only 150 million private vehicles in China for 800 million urban residents, that is, 18 ones for every 100 urban residents and less than a quarter of the figure in the USA Yet, it would be totally unrealistic for us to expand the car population from today's 50 to 500 million based on the existing road resources. Hence, we have identified an alternative: increasing car usage through better sharing instead of putting more cars on road.

Third, the internet platform is a prerequisite for the development of sharing economy.

Without the internet platform, there wouldn't have been the necessary condition for the development of sharing economy. All sharing exercises are arranged now via the internet. Before the internet birth, carpooling was done only among neighbors or by posting signs by a road. There were neither viable platforms nor organization plans, but very high transaction costs. It is the advent of mobile internet that enables the intelligent matching between the supply and demands, eliminating the problem of information asymmetry. Meanwhile, the bottlenecks in the transportation industry make sharing economy entrenched in this field and gain quick traction.

Fourth, China will be among the fastest-growing and largest sharing economies.

In stark contrast to the USA, it is very expensive owning a private car, while relatively cheap using taxi service in China. In most cases, it is the poor in the USA that drive their own cars while the rich take a taxi. The opposite is the case with China, where even newly-graduated office workers will rush to have their own cars once they can afford one rather than taking a taxi. Thanks to its various advantages, including affordability and cost-effectiveness, more and more people and cars will sign up for ride-sharing platforms like Didi. The difference between sharing economy and ownership economy in terms of cost-effectiveness will drive more users to shift to those ride-sharing platforms faster. So, I believe that it is very likely that China will be among the fastest-growing and largest sharing economies in the world.

Furthermore, the rising campaign of Mass Entrepreneurship and Innovation in China will enter a new stage in 2016. With capital and talent markets becoming more and more mature while the entrepreneurship thresholds get lower and lower, more startups will try their luck in sharing economy. Huge user demands, frugal cultural traditions, and early successful practices all signify that sharing economy will have an infinite development space in China.

Nowadays, many Chinese Internet enterprises have led the world, demonstrating the strong Chinese innovation and entrepreneurship in the sharing economy era and taking pride in the national industry development. Going forward, we will make concerted effort to forge a "market and an innovation-led and user-oriented community with a shared future, which interconnects and is shared and governed by businesses and the government" for fulfilling our common aspiration for having the internet technology empower national development and social progress and building China into a real world-class internet power.

The sharing economy era is coming. To seize such an epochal opportunity and respond proactively to challenges of the world is the responsibility of every internet enterprise.

Cheng Wei
Founder & CEO of Didi Chuxing
Beijing, China

Foreword by Guo Kaitian: Sharing Economy—Shed Lights on Economic Surplus

Western economic theories need to be revolutionized. "Rational Economic Man" has been one of the fundamental assumptions in western economics since Adam Smith touched on "egoism" in his "*The Wealth of Nations*" (Adam Smith, 1776). Being taken as the embodiment of pursuing the maximization of individual interests, the rational economic man believes that self-interest is the natural instinct of humans, simply pursuing his own interests at the expense of others' and collective interests.

However, such an assumption about "egoism" has no longer held water in the context of sharing economy. On the emerging Internet platform, people no longer regard ownership as the best way to obtain products. No longer emphasizing the ownership of products or services by means of purchase, they value the way of thinking of cooperative sharing more, preferring the temporary access to products or services or sharing them with others. The expression "access over ownership" is the most concise description of sharing economy, though being far from all the hallmarks of sharing economy.

We know that supply and demand are the two aspects of an economic contradiction. Catalyzed by sharing economy, they are connected on a large scale but in a different way now—this is one of the latest developments. Unlike traditional economies, the connection is based on economic surplus, which shows up at the enterprise level as idle inventory and capacity and at the individual level as idle funds, items, and time, namely, spare money, articles, and time.

To put economic surplus to work is a new approach to increase social wealth.

In the past, economic surpluses existed fragmentarily in all areas of society; and it tended to take a tremendous cost but marginal social value to integrate them. But now, the case is completely different. With various innovative models of sharing economy, a large number of economic surpluses here and there across the entire society are integrated for reconnecting and matching the supply and demands, thus producing new economic benefits.

As a result, the realization of "bringing all to full play and make the best use of all things" gives a new momentum to macroeconomic development.

Why can personal resources be shared in sharing economy? Tencent WeStart is working on a mode for start-ups—sharing industrial ecological resources. To be specific, WeStart centered on common needs from enterprises has pro-growth elements, including network platform traffics, technologies, products, office spaces, hardware/software devices, investments, media resources, and others, shared among them so as to let entrepreneurs focus their efforts on their core missions, such as product development and business operations, thus virtually eliminating the issue of operation and service resources staying idle.

Besides in business communities, the sharing economy also thrives in the public service sector. Nowadays, major countries well aware of the high effectiveness and efficiency of sharing economy in resource allocation have placed an increasing emphasis on developing sharing economy, thus clarifying the strategic position of sharing economy and working out policies to encourage its development. For example, the British Government in 2014 outlined its development plan for sharing economy with a view on developing England into a global hub of sharing economy; the South Korean government proposed to build a "Demonstration City" of developing the sharing economy; and the European Union also rolled out its guidelines for developing the sharing economy.

The sharing economy is a profound economic revolution. Advancing the traditional value of decentralization, the mentality of cooperative sharing has become the leading idea underlying business development, delivering a tremendous effect on resource reallocation, organizational restructuring, supply-demand rematch, and even governance pattern reshape in the whole society. As Robin Chase put it, sharing for all is driving the transformation of this industrialized society into a sharing economy one.

Though the sharing economy is being in full swing, the value of sharing economy has not been fully brought out in China yet. Nowadays, the sustained expansion of effective domestic demands and accelerating the supply-side reform are becoming two important means to fuel the national economic development, and sharing economy has been increasingly demonstrated its great potential for rebuilding a more efficient and sustainable new supply-demand relationship.

First of all, sharing economy offers everyone the chance to participate in the historical process of supply-side reform. Thanks to the development of mobile Internet and the rapid prevalence of smartphones, and high-speed wireless networks, the autonomy of individuals is ever increasingly emphasized. As a result, everyone can be both an aggregator and a disseminator of information or both an employer and an employee. Enterprises in emerging sharing economy are no longer about producing goods but rather about providing information and trading platforms.

Next, the sharing between enterprises is conducive to slashing costs and improving efficiency. With the in-depth integration of the internet and traditional industries, a batch of innovative sharing economy platforms are emerging and winning wide recognition from consumers and markets. According to rough estimates, sharing economy exceeded RMB 1 trillion in scale in China in 2015; and it is expanding beyond travel and accommodation to all areas of personal consumption. Meanwhile, the enterprise end market is also gradually taking shape.

Such a boom of sharing economy has had an effect on hundreds of millions of people. It can be predicted that it will rebuild the connections between individuals, between individuals and businesses, and between businesses, and enhance the operating efficiency of the entire society and economy, conductive to boosting China's economy to accelerate the realization of shifting to new drivers and building a more humane society in China.

Guo Kaitian
President of Tencent Research Institute
Shenzhen, China

Preface: Sharing Economy—Provide New Driving Forces for Economic Development

In 2015, China achieved the historic goal of "Double Over-the-Half" in economic growth and social progress: the service sector's proportion in the GDP rose to 50.5%, over the 50% mark for the first time, and internet penetration to 50.3% in the society, marking consumption has replaced investment as the main engine of economic growth, and the Internet-enabled new economy has gradually dominated mainstream consumer markets.

2015, the inaugural year of Internet Plus, witnessed internet gaining further traction among all the walks of life, and the waves of innovation and entrepreneurship surging over time in IoT, cloud computing, big data, and other emerging technologies. Those mass efforts played the role of the finishing shot in our process of striving for the goal of "Double Over-the-Half".

During the 2015 NPC and CPPCC Sessions, I put forward a proposal: *Promoting Internet Plus-Driven Economic and Social Innovation and Development*, in the hope of carving out new growth fields and fostering new ecologies by integrating the internet with various industries (incl. traditional ones) through internet platforms, information and communication technologies. At the 2016 NPC and CPPCC Sessions, I once again submitted a bill, together with the other four, on that topic: *Promoting Sharing Economy Development to Provide New Momentum to Economic Growth*. Admittedly, with the consistent relationship of call and response with "Internet Plus", sharing economy is, in essence, a new form of

"Internet Plus" application and popularization in various industries; and thus, it has the functions in eliminating information asymmetry, slashing transaction costs, and improving labor productivity. After making efforts for one year or so, "Internet Plus" has completed its initial preparations. With the foundation laid, it has been poised to seek further development in certain vertical sectors of significant scales and fraught with growth constrains, such as education, health care, and transportation. So, sharing economy could likely be a main form and mode of integration between "Internet Plus" and those traditional industries.

Though failing to be significant enough to define an era, sharing economy, indeed, offers an important opportunity for economic transformation and upgrading. On the one hand, many new entities sprang up over the past a couple of years in some sectors, for example, travel and leasing, creating a large number of jobs. Although such new entities are in different industries and areas, they all have a common characteristic: a brand-new and innovative economy mode in re-matching the supply and demand of social surplus resources, including labor, services, goods. On the other hand, developing sharing economy has also gained the global awareness and even landed on the development agendas in various major countries, for example, China's *2016 Report on the Work of the Government* and the *Outline of the 13th Five-year Plan*, and the government literature in Britain, France, South Korea, etc.

The global rise of sharing economy is not an accident but a new mode arising from the booming O2O (Online to Offline) sector, expanding the internet industry and even the transition of the broad Chinese economy into a new normal. Although it is still in its infancy, sharing economy has already shown its strong explosive power, vitality, and capability in promoting the interconnection of things rapidly.

Achievements in Mobile Internet Development

Over the past couple of years, a raft of sharing economy entities, for example, Airbnb and Didi, have risen rapidly. According to incomplete statistics, the global market of sharing economy in 2015 was approximately USD 810.0 billion in scale and that in China more than RMB 1.0 trillion. Simply out of an idea on paper, sharing economy has already grown into a raging economic and social tide sweeping across the globe. Such an explosive development of sharing economy is largely attributed to its three distinct features:

First of all, sharing economy is about the socialized reuse of idle resources. Sharing resources, such as time, space, and items, among large numbers of users can improve their use efficiency, realize their maximal market values, give more concession and convenience to their consumers, and generate additional incomes to their owners. Sharing economy enterprises integrate a large number of idle resources in a society to achieve a situation benefiting all the market players (suppliers, owners, and demanders).

Secondly, sharing economy broadened the sharing relationship limited to acquaintances to larger groups of strangers and strengthened mutual trust among members in a society. Sharing economy is a business form grown out of acquaintance relationships, and goes beyond acquaintance trust to commercial trust on the strength of the well-developed mobile internet technology. In this new business mode, building on the spirit of sharing and the convenience brought by the internet, participants have "sitting still" resources in the society to move again through aligned actions and redistribute social resources on demand in the society, truly realizing the desirable vision of "Access over Ownership".

Thirdly, sharing economy facilitates the shift from centralized mass production to decentralized personalized customization. In stark contrast to the modes marked by "centralized and standardized mass production", the past two industrial revolutions sought to establish, sharing economy's decentralized value network places more emphasis on providing personalized products and services. With individuals being both consumers and producers, innovation vitality in each one is fully brought out. That is, sharing economy can truly motivate and empower all the elements in the society, and thus achieve the effectiveness of "bringing all ones to full play and make the best use of all things".

Overall, sharing economy is also the inevitable product of mobile internet technology development at today's stage. The development of mobile internet and the popularization of intelligent terminals have enabled the wide interconnection of participants, mobile payment and location-based service have made sharing easier and faster, and networking and big data analysis technologies have enabled accurate and efficient matching between supply and demand of resources, greatly reducing the cost of fragmented transactions between participants. Besides, as social networks and credit evaluation mechanisms are maturing, new trust relationships are established. The development of sharing economy has also led to the emergence of super-connected networks, where the connections between peoples, between people and things, and between things and things are strengthened through the reuse of social idle resources.

Accelerating the Shifting to New Drivers Behind Economic Development

At present, China's economy has entered a new normal: economic growth has slowed down from high-speed rates to medium/high-speed rates, the population is aging, consumption has played an increasing role in the economy but there still exist the overcapacity and a lack of effective supply. Now, sharing economy has become a national strategy, and to develop sharing economy has been repeatedly touched on in various government documents, including the *Communique of the Fifth Plenary Session of the 18th CPC Central Committee* and the *Outline of the 13th Five-Year Plan.*

In his important remarks on the world economy themed "Innovative Growth that Benefits All" at the 10th Summit of the Group of Twenty Major Economies in Antalya on November 15, 2015, Chinese President Xi Jinping stated that the new round of scientific and industrial revolution is creating historic opportunities; and he cited sharing economy as an important innovation case in promoting reform and innovation.[1]

When addressing the 2015 Summer Davos Forum in Dalian, Chinese Premier Li Keqiang also endorsed the role of sharing economy and pointed out that "The sharing economy that is thriving on a global scale now opens a new way to drive the economic growth. Entrepreneurship and innovation through sharing and collaboration lower the threshold and costs and increase the speed of doing business. This opens up space for developing the sharing economy in China and may get a lot of people involved".[2]

In fact, sharing economy has already demonstrated its remarkable effectiveness in promoting economic transformation and shifting to new drivers of growth.

[1] Additional Readings: http://news.xinhuanet.com/politics/2015-11/16/c_1117147101.htm.

[2] Additional Readings: http://news.xinhuanet.com/fortune/2015-09/10/c_128215895.htm.

First of all, sharing economy helps solve the problem of economic surplus in some regions and industries in China. Take the domestic real estate market as an example. According to the statistics from China National Information Center, the total floor area of unsold commercial housing across the country increased from 216 million square meters at the end of 2010 to more than 686 million square meters in November 2015, with an average annual growth rate of more than 30%, so reducing the inventory in the real estate sector has remained a daunting task. According to the sharing economy thinking, there are at least two ways to destock relatively quickly: one is, sharing economy platforms cooperate with developers in disposing of unsold houses, providing value added services to developers and facilitating the handover of unsold properties; and the other is, sharing economy platforms rent out these unsold houses, meeting rental needs by connecting and matching developers, owners and consumers and reusing the long idle properties.

Second, sharing economy can also be an effective means of pushing on supply-side reform, becoming a driving force behind the growth of the service sector and substantially facilitating the structural economic adjustment. First, sharing economy can turn idle inventory resources into new supplies through socialized internet platforms. For example, private houses, vehicles, funds, knowledge, experience, skills, and other resources can be used to match supply and demand on a large scale across the whole society at lower transaction costs. Second, consumer demand can be effectively expanded. Some sharing platforms in the catering sector turn potential consumers into actual ones by means of sharing their personal experiences, thus triggering experience or taste-oriented consumption and increasing the willingness of customers to buy services.

Besides, sharing economy can effectively expand employment, promote mass entrepreneurship and innovation, and increase residents' incomes. According to incomplete statistics, platforms in online employment, crowd-sourcing, express services, and other emerging sectors have created more than 30 million full-time and part-time job openings. A June 2015 survey by the School of New Media, Peking University shows that nearly 3 million jobs have been created by Didi platform through its taxi service, tailored taxi service, fast-ride service, substitute driving service, and test driving service.

Nowadays, China's sharing economy is expanding beyond transportation and accommodation sectors into multiple segments of personal consumption, and the enterprise end market is also gradually taking shape, providing conditions for green and sustainable development. It is foreseeable that sharing economy trend, which has affected hundreds of millions of people, will inject a powerful new driving force into China's economic growth and help the Chinese economy shift into new areas of growth, turning the service sector into the main engine of economic growth.

An Era of Greater Connectivity Is Coming

However, the booming sharing economy also faces various constraints and challenges in many aspects, including regulation, supply, and benefit adjustment.

Related regulation is yet to be improved to keep pace with time. Now, China is still stuck in the traditional method of imposing regulation by regions and sectors, adopting the systems of prior approval and market access. But in the sharing economy era, new multisectoral forms of business are springing up like mushrooms. Uncovered by the traditional segmented management mode, most of such forms are prone to being illegalized at any time. So when it comes to new business forms and models in sharing economy, rather than following impractical approaches to force new developments to fit with outdated frameworks, regulators should adapt their regulation tactics to local realities on a case-by-case basis, timely revising or removing unreasonable rules and regulations to promote the development of sharing economy.

The benefit adjustments caused by innovation make overall planning and coordination even more complicated. Especially in the travel and accommodation sectors, sharing economy with its tangible cost advantage and brand-new business models puts huge pressure on traditional enterprises in related sectors, thus inevitably incurring challenges and backlashes. Yet, on the other hand, we also see too many examples of sharing economy merging with traditional entities. For instance, Lincoln Motor Company partners with CustomMade (a designer's online communication platform) manufacturers in designing high-end automotive jewelry, Walgreens works with TaskRabbit (a task poster community website) in delivering prescription drugs to clients, and Home Depot employs Uber for delivering Christmas trees. Over time, there will be more such cases of sharing economy being incorporated into traditional enterprises.

Insufficient infrastructure limits the mass participation. Being a product of highly developed internet, sharing economy is widely found in both urban and rural areas across the country. However, the network infrastructure needs to be further improved. First of all, about half of the population in China still can't get direct access to the internet, especially the disabled, the elderly, and residents in relatively remote and poor regions. We should give them the opportunity to get integrated into the mobile internet world and enjoy the benefits of sharing economy. Second, the 4G/3G mobile internet services should be popularized quickly in those backwater areas. In addition, the internet charges are still at higher levels and such charges should be sharply reduced.

In the long run, sharing economy is simply a phased achievement in the development process of mobile internet. Along with progress made in technology, changing ideas, and updated business modes, there will come new forms and new models. Everything may be connected beyond our present imagination, and exploration and practice hold the key to the progress of human beings.

Shenzhen, China

Ma Huateng
Zhang Xiaorong
Sun Yi
Cai Xiongshan

Contents

List of Figures

List of Tables

PART I

Theory: An Innovative Practice

Preface: Sharing Economy Isn't the Share Economy

Where was sharing economy originated? For any new thing, we tend to trace back to its source. We find out that sharing economy, one of the most talked-about topics all over the world, is not the "share economy" in the eyes of academic scholars in the past at all. What's going on there?

The research on the share (sharing) economy as a new concept began as early as in the 1970s or the 1980s. Professor Li Bingyan, a Chinese economist, articulated the core points of the socialist share economy theory for the first time at home and abroad in his articles: *A Preliminary Exploration of the Category of Socialist Costs* (1981) and *Labor Remuneration isn't Part of Product Cost* (1982). In 1984, Martin Lawrence Weitzman, a US economist, also proposed the share economy theory in his book *The Share Economy: Conquering Stagflation.*

In their theories, both scholars focused on enterprise behaviors at the micro-level, explored the factors behind the insufficient economic forces in the distribution field, and advocated for some new systems of benefit sharing and fiscal and taxation policies so as to establish new structures and mechanism of stimulating economies, eliminate traditional contradictions of interests, and solve the problem of insufficient economic development momentous. In essence, the core is to study how to distribute the profits of their businesses between workers and capitalists.

Obviously, sharing economy at the center of today's talking points around the world is not share economy touched on by the two economists, but an emerging economic phenomenon and a socialized Business Model that integrates highly developed Internet technologies.

Being based on social sharing, is it equivalent to information sharing based on socialized mass production? In his book: *The Wealth of Networks* in 2002, Yochai·Benkler, a professor at Harvard Law School and Director at Berkman Center for Internet &Society at Harvard University (a world-renowned network research center), coined the phrase of "commons-based peer production" to expand on his thought of socialized production. In his view, employing network technology for socialized production can solve the issues related to the rational utilization of resources, and in the information age, the non-marketized and non-specialized production activities by individuals and/or loosely or closely-connected cooperators will have an increasing role in our society.

It sounds to have a hue of "sharing". Unfortunately, Prof. Benkler's thought focuses on explaining such cases as Wikipedia, open-source software, and blogospheres, which are just not typical of sharing economy. In other words, they are simply "sharing", not "sharing economy".

And then, what exactly is sharing economy?

At this point, we need to have a brand-new concept—collaborative consumption (or cooperative consumption).

Collaborative consumption, literally, is a group consumption pattern where numerous consumers spend as a group and thus have a much stronger bargaining advantage relative to that for individual spenders. The term was coined by Marcus·Felson, a professor in Sociology at Texas State University, and Joe L. Spaeth, a professor in Sociology at University of Illinois, in their co-authored paper in 1978: *Community Structure and Collaborative Consumption: A Routine Activity Approach*. Collaborative consumption was, then, also "cooperative consumption".

In 2007, Ray Algar, a management consultant at Oxygen Consultancy, used the term "collaborative consumption" in his paper: *Collaborative Consultation*, and found that it was a latest global rage, where consumers exchanged goods and services via websites, including eBay and Gumtree (the top classified info site in the U.K.), share their accommodation experiences via Trip Advisor (a world-renowned travel community), and share (take the ownership of) big-ticket items like cars, real estates, and airplanes by pooling their purchasing powers. It is just in that paper that he highlighted the factor: sharing.

Over time, collaborative consumption took on richer meanings. For example, Baidu Baike defined collaborative consumption as an economic model where via online and/or offline communities (teams or groups), salons, training sessions, and other means, consumers get "connected" to enable cooperation or mutually beneficial consumption, including the cooperation in possessing, leasing, using or exchanging goods and services, pooling procurement and doing other transactions.

Further then, in 2011, the Times cited "collaborative consumption" among the top ten innovative ideas that may revolutionize the world.

In 2013–2014, the Economist published several articles on the development of sharing economy in the USA, especially problems and opportunities that such companies as Airbnb and Uber met with each other in their business model development.

The fire was flaring up further with governments stepping in. Among them, the U.K. appeared to be the most aggressive and the most ambitious and drew out a vision in 2015 to build Britain into the world's most suitable destination for entrepreneurship, investment, and development. To that end, it enacted a series of policies to promote the development of sharing economy, making it an important driving force for economic development.

Identifying its origin is not to speak like a book, but to get a better understanding of its fundamentals and proactively respond to its possible trends by drawing on its evolution process. Through the in-depth look into its history, we can obviously find that the relation between collaborative consumption and sharing economy is almost like the two sides of a coin. But sharing economy has reached out much farther and much wider beyond regions and social forms, and it has developed into an internet tech-enabled revolution around the globe. It is guiding the development of global economies, changing our lifestyles, and ushering us into the future.

CHAPTER 1

Demystify Sharing Economy

Many scholars and institutions believe that sharing economy has a similar connotation to those of collaborative consumption, on-demand economy, gig economy, and so on. However, if you take a closer look, you'll find that sharing economy, indeed, has some overlaps with them but actually, they're horses of different colors, albeit seemingly similar outwardly.

The True Nature of Collaborative Consumption

Rachel·Botsman believes that sharing economy is collaborative consumption. She illustrated her point in a co-authored book: ***What's Mine Is Yours: the Rise of Collaborative Consumption***, which means in Chinese 我的就是你的：协同消费的崛起 and the Chinese version of which is entitled as《共享经济时代：互联网思维下的协同消费商业模式》. In the book, she argued that collaborative consumption is a brand-new business model emerging in the Internet world. To simply put it, consumers can share products and services with others in a cooperative manner without having to get the ownership of them. Looking from the standing point of consumers, such a definition is to lay emphasis on collaboration, in essence, sharing though it also especially makes the point that the objects to be shared are products and services.

Rachel·Botsman holds that "secondary trading" is also a typical pattern in sharing economy. Secondary trading is to reuse idle second-hand

M. Huateng et al., *The Chinese Sharing Economy*,
https://doi.org/10.1007/978-981-33-6494-3_1

resources through resale and thus improves their efficiency. Accordingly, she concluded that collaborative consumption comes in three forms.

The first form is a product-service system, namely, owners rent out their personal belongings standing idle - cars, houses, etc., to get extra incomes.

The second one is the redistribution market, namely the venue for trading secondhand items. The representative venues include Freecycle (an idle item donation platform in the USA), which doles out all kinds of articles free of charge, internet-based sales websites like eBay and Gumtree, and some forums that are licensed to exchange idle items.

The third one is a collaborative lifestyle, namely, numerous individuals of similar needs and interests gather to share or exchange relatively nonphysical resources, such as time, space, and skills. The most representative of them is the so-called "Time Bank".

The research team under Juho Hamari at Tampere University of Technology in Finland shared such a view. The team conducted a study on collaborative consumption in sharing economy by analyzing 254 platforms and concluded that these behaviors on platforms could be classified into two types: access to ownership and transfer of ownership, with the former meaning that owners provide and share goods and services within a prescribed time-frame, for example, renting out or lending out their belongings, while the latter including exchanging, donating or purchasing secondhand items. The team published its research findings in a paper titled *Sharing Economy: Why Do People Participate in Collaborative Consumption?*

Their view has gained traction among an even larger audience. One report on the German sharing economy: *The Phenomenon of the Sharing Economy in Germany: Consumer Motivations for Participating in Collaborative Consumption Schemes* also classified and defined sharing economy based on the concept of Rachel·Botsman, and it went even further to argue that besides P2P (pair-to-pair) services, sharing economy also consists of product-service systems and redistribution markets: first, to enable customers to use products while the providers keep the ownership; second, to cover the markets for handing over new or secondhand items; and third, to provide on-demand services to rally individuals for tasks.

In its report: *Circular Economy Innovation & New Business Models Initiative*, Global Young Leaders Conference of the World Economic Forum also holds that sharing economy, together with collaborative consumption, consists of three systems: redistribution markets, e.g., eBay, Craigslist (a leading free classified advertising site), Swap.com(a leading mother & baby products commission sale platform), thredUP(a used children's articles commission sale platform), Yerdle (a platform for sharing used articles); Product-Service Systems, e.g., Zipcar (an online car rental firm), Snapgoods (a community rental service website), CarShare (a car-sharing platform); Collaborative lifestyles, e.g., Airbnb, Skillshare (a skill-sharing website), LiquidSpace (a platform providing office space for frequent travelers).

To touch on collaborative consumption, Zipcar Founder Robin Chase wrote a book: *Sharing Economy (People Inc.: How People and Platforms Are Inventing the Collaborative Economy and Reinventing Capitalism).* As to the phrase, collaborative economy was wrongly translated into the Chinese equivalent: 分享经济 (namely: sharing economy in English) in its Chinese version. But Robin Chase maintains that collaboration is the core concept she wants to convey in that book, and sharing is just a necessary link in the process of collaboration. By now, it can be concluded that collaboration and sharing have the same fundamental direction.

Emphasis on the Perspective of "Labor"

Besides, there may be many other expressions for sharing economy. Such expressions interpret the connotation of sharing economy from different perspectives and contribute to our deeper and more comprehensive understanding of sharing economy.

For example, the U.S news website the Daily Beast came up with the notion of the gig economy (part-time work) for the first time in its op-ed article on January 12, 2009, titled the *Gig Economy*. Isn't doing gig work the sharing of an individual's spare time? To provide services or do different "tasks" in exchange for incomes by making use of an individual's spare time and skills is also known as moonlighting or doing a part-time job. As a result, in a presidential campaign speech, the Democratic candidate Ms. Hillary Clinton also meant sharing economy model by saying gig economy. The word gig refers to any jobs, careers, or tasks. This definition articulates the newly-added meaning of sharing economy: online job hiring. To put it in other words, through socialized platforms, individuals get more flexible job openings for providing particular services within particular time frames and are no longer permanently employed by an organization or institution.

Aspen Institute, the leading think tank in modern USA, argues that despite having no standardized definition, sharing economy usually refers to the economic activities that promote exchanges of goods, assets, and services among individuals or different sets of dynamic domains through technology platforms. In the working paper: the *Future of Work in the Sharing Economy*, one of its report series themed *Economic Opportunities: Working in America*, the think tank classified the sharing economy entities into two groups: sharing economy entities promoting exchanges of properties or space and those promoting exchanges of labor.

First group promotes exchanges of properties or space: renting out a room or a house (Airbnb), letting out cars (Relay Rides and Getaround) or bicycles (Liquid).

Second group promotes exchanges of labor: hitching or sharing a ride (Uber and Lyft), providing on-demand labor suitable for various tasks (TaskRabbit), house cleaning and maintenance (Handy), and on-demand food delivery services (Instacart).

Ms. Benita Matofska, founder of the People Who Share and an avid practitioner of sharing economy, gave a richer definition. In the light of her many years of practice experience, she defined sharing economy (also known as P2P economy, collaborative economy, and cooperative economy) as a socioeconomic ecosystem based on sharing humans and materials, including the sharing of means of production, products, distribution channels, and goods/services in the process of trading or consumption between different users or organizations. Such a system may come in numerous forms, and it usually includes information technologies needed to enable individuals, legal persons, and non-profit organizations to share, distribute, and reuse redundant goods or services. A common premise is that when the information about an item is shared, the item will gain more commercial values to individuals or organizations.

A Broad Perspective

The report: *Is Sharing Really Caring? A Nuanced Introduction to the Peer Economy* released in 2014 by the Center for Civic Media at MIT broke down sharing economy into the following categories:

1. Peer-to-peer market places: It is also known as P2P economy, using online markets as the rallying venues to match transactions between

providers and consumers, the cases in point include Airbnb, Etsy, Getaround, Shapeways, Uber, and Lyft;

2. Gift economy: service spaces: It is an entity in the gift economy describes the practice of giving gifts as "an arrangement for transferring goods or services". For example, serial software developers at Nintendo distribute codes to their fans free of charge. Other examples include tool libraries, fan fictions, etc.;
3. Commons-based peer production: It is related to small-ticket "products" from inputs by numerous volunteers, such as Wikipedia, etc. In general, the motivation for participation is social recognition and personal fulfillment. Other examples include open source software, hacker groups, etc.;
4. Solidarity economy/democratic wealth: The communities are housekeepers, and wealth is usually used for mutual assistance. The wealth and capital here are not limited to money, such as Time Bank, etc.;
5. Collaborative consumption: It refers to an economy and society that aims at zero production, such as Zipcar, community parks, bicycle sharing, etc.;
6. P2P lending: It includes small loans, purchases of debt assets, etc. For example, P2P platforms like Lending Club and Neighborly;
7. Crowd-funding: It covers such crowd-funding platforms as DonorsChoose, Patreon, Kickstarter, and IndieGoGo;
8. Ridesharing.

Ownership and Access

Compared with the broad perspective, there is a specialized perspective as well. Jeremy Rifkin articulated the concept of access economy in his book: the *Age of Access*. Such a statement refers to one of the most important features of sharing economy, namely, access goes before ownership. People will no longer pursue ownership of goods or assets in the future, but just be content with how to use it. For example, I don't have to own a car. It will be, all the same, okay for me to just use it for a short trip, so I don't have to hold it all the time.

A lot of scholars in China agree with Rifkin's theory as it came into China so early that it has been so deeply entrenched in the country so it eclipsed all the other doctrines. Jeremy Rifkin is a US economic and social critic, an orator, and President of the Foundation on Economic Trends in Washington, DC. He is also the guide of many unicorns in sharing economy, including Uber and Airbnb. Two of his books, *Third Industrial Revolution* and *Zero Marginal Cost Society*[1] command large batches of Chinese followers. *Zero Marginal Cost Society* makes three major predictions about the future of the world: The cooperative economy, or sharing economy, will disrupt the work at many large international companies; the existing energy systems and structures will be replaced by the energy internet; and the upcoming machine revolution will wipe off many of our current jobs. The book refines some key ideas in the *Age of Access* and went viral upon the release of its Chinese version in China. Yet, it provides no new insight other than the existing ones on sharing economy.

Economical Model Theory

According to certain current symptoms in sharing economy, other scholars and institutions define sharing economy as an economic model of re-matching supply and demands. PwC, for example, noted in the report entitled *Sharing Economy: Consumer Intelligence Series* that as an economic model, sharing economy distinguishes itself from simple sharing in that: (1) digital platforms connect idle capacity and demands; and (2) trading extends beyond ownership to achieve more options and lower costs, including rental, lending, subscription, resale, exchange, donation; (3) more forms of collaborative consumption; (4) brand experience and emotional ties; and (5) trust-based behaviors. PwC further stated in the report that sharing economy enabled individuals and groups to gain from underutilized assets. Physical assets are converted into services this way, for example, the owner of an idle vehicle may allow others to rent his car, or the owner of the apartment may rent out his idle apartment while he is on holiday.

JoSanKu, Founder of Kozaza (a rental website of homestay facilities in South Korea), defined sharing economy as an economic model of getting access to products rather than owning them by the means of sharing, exchanging, trading or renting in its report *Sharing Economy*. He argues that sharing economy is a relatively broad term for obtaining social, economic, environmental, political, and spiritual benefits by sharing both

[1] The Third Industrial Revolution and The Zero Marginal Cost Society have been published on May 2012 and November 2014 by CITIC Press House.—Editor.

physical and non-physical resources, such as time, knowledge, capital, and natural resources with others.

The Fraunhofer-Gesellschaft (Fraunhofer IAO) defines sharing economy as a practical and economic model of enabling individuals and companies to share products, services and experiences through technologies and communities in its report: *Sharing Economy in Urban Environments*.

The report *User Reputation: Building Trust and Addressing Privacy Issues in the Sharing Economy* describes sharing economy as an economic mode based on human and physical resources which can be exchanged between two persons by means of borrowing or renting goods or services needed.

Jiang Qiping noted that a new A2A (Application to Application) internet mode will be widely employed in the future. "The core feature of A2A is point-to-point applications, that is, the point-to-point collaboration between applications," he said. The A2A feature stands apart from others in that self-organization, self-coordination, and self-adaption complex and intelligent business ecology can be formed bottom-up among web applications independent from the central platform. A2A will have higher requirements on commercial ecological structures, providing public goods by means of web pages rather than the platforms, and eventually leading the broad economy to shift to the sharing economy model characterized by non-possession.

Circular Economy Perspective

Another research perspective on sharing economy is based on the circular economy. In its report: Circular Economy Innovation & New Business Models Initiative, Global Young Leaders Summit of the World Economic Forum noted that sharing economy is a complement to circular economy. On the other hand, both sharing economy and collaborative consumption can free up idle capacities—untapped social, economic, and environmental valuable resources and underutilized assets for reallocation through technology platforms.

In his report: Debating the Sharing Economy, Juliet Schor broke down sharing economy activities into 4 categories: recycling, improving utilization of durable assets, exchanging services, and sharing productive assets.

The first category is recycling, and its typical entities include eBay and Craigslist in earlier times, thredUp and Threadflip (a second-hand boutique clothing trading platform) since 2010, free exchange sites, such as Freecycle and Yerdle, and barter sites, such as Swapstyle.com;

The second category is the promotion of the pooling and use of durable goods and other assets to enhance their utilization, and its typical entities include Zipcar in the transportation sector, car-rental websites, such as Relay Rides, carpooling services, such as Zimride, taxi services, such as Uber, UberX and Lyft, bicycle-sharing services, such as Hubway in Boston and Divvy Bikes in Chicago, and Couchsurfing and Airbnb in the accommodation sector;

The third category is service exchange, and its typical entities include Time Bank in earlier times, and TaskRabbit and Zaarly;

The fourth category is the sharing of productive assets for the purpose of production rather than consumption, and its typical entities include Hackerspace, Makerspaces, Skillshare.com, and Peer-to-peer University.

Definition Based on Four Elements

The definition of sharing economy varies with different persons. How can we have a more intuitive understanding of it? Some studies found that many scholars and institutions define sharing economy more or less based on four elements: individuals, idleness (surplus), network platforms, and benefits.

For example, in its latest report: *Sharing Economy in the U.K.*, the British Office of Government Commerce points out that sharing economy consists of trading platforms which bring individuals together and connect demand and supply. The participants in sharing economy in earlier times were motivated by potential benefits (including social and environmental benefits) from less consumption and more cooperation. This definition involves individuals, platforms, and benefits.

"Sharing economy means the direct exchange of goods and services between individuals, including sharing cars, sharing rooms, exchanging idle items. All of which can be done through networks," says Nancy Koehn, a professor of business management at Harvard Business School. The three elements mentioned here are individuals, idleness, and networks.

In his book: *How People and Platforms Are Inventing the Collaborative Economy and Reinventing Capitalism*, Robin Chase argues that

Surplus Capacity + Sharing Platform + Mass Participation lead to a brand-new "Mass Share" pattern, where organizational advantages (size and resources) and personal advantages (localization, specialization, and customization) are integrated to enable resource abundance in a resource-scarce context. In such a definition, the emphasis is placed on three elements: surplus, individuals, and platforms.

In their book: *Sharing Economy: An In-depth Look at its Evolution & Trajectory Across Industries*, Michael J. Olson, and Samuel J. Kemp hold that sharing economy arises from individuals pursuit of reduced costs and earned profits by individuals. Sharing economy is a market, where (1) users are individuals, enterprises or institutions; (2) oversupplied and shared assets or skills create economic benefits for allocators and users; and (3) networks facilitate and enable communication and coordination for sharing oversupplied and shared assets or skills. Four elements: individuals, surplus, benefits and networks are emphasized here to varying degrees.

In China, in their paper titled *A Study on the Development Path of Sharing Economy in China*, Ling Chao, and Zhang Zan, PhD candidates at School of Management, Fudan University, said: "Sharing economy, known as the P2P model, is largely transactions in which natural persons lease their goods through platforms (usually internet platforms)." Such a definition involves two elements: individuals and platforms.

Liu Guohua and Wu Bo highlight the element—Internet, and further argue that mobile terminals + "Internet Plus" + Efficient Activation of Existing Users + Mass Participation = Sharing Economy 2.0 in their book: *Sharing Economy 2.0: Disruptive Change in Individuals, Business and Society*.

The list of such definitions is long.

Tencent Research Institute gives a more intuitive definition: sharing economy refers to the economic phenomenon that the public shares their idle resources with others on socialized platforms for generating incomes. Such a definition includes all the four elements: first, the phrase "the public" mainly means individuals for the time being (it may extend its scope to cover enterprises, governments, and other entities in the future, but the form should remain mainly limited to P2P); second, the phrase "idle resources" mainly refers to private items, such as funds, houses, and cars, and personal knowledge, skills and experience; third, the phrase "socialized platforms" mainly refers to the platforms enabling massive sharing via internet technology; and fourth, the phrase "generating incomes" mainly means generating incomes by means of three basic models: network leasing, network secondary trading, and doing network odd work, which are also the basic sharing models. In other words, without any one or more of the four elements, it may not be sharing economy we are talking about here.

It is important to note that the three models mentioned here are mainly about individual participants. Globally, enterprises and governments have also been involved in the game, so the connotation of sharing economy will be further enriched.

For sure, it is still difficult to grasp the essence of sharing economy accurately. In an era of global innovation, sharing economy can take on richer meanings at any time.

Except for the researchers' statistics, a precise definition doesn't make much. Despite being a little broad, the definition by Tencent Research Institute hit the nail right on the head in that it clarifies the four fundamental elements of sharing economy: individuals, resources, platforms, and incomes. We deeply hope that there will be more accurate definitions in the future.

CHAPTER 2

The Gene of Four Business Models

Sharing economy isn't the practice that is exclusively limited to sharing among individuals. Sharing among individuals is only its mainstream form at the current stage, and other forms of sharing, including sharing among enterprises, may emerge over time. Briefly, by the nature of main agents - suppliers and demanders, we have four basic business models in sharing economy: C2C (Consumer-to-consumer), C2B (Customer to Business), B2B (Business to Business) and B2C (Business to Customer). Yet, it's worth noting that these four models all carry obvious Internet genes, emphasizing that each of the suppliers and demanders directly participates in transactions, that is, P2P. So the common gene of the four models is decentralization and disintermediation. In that book, it can be roughly understood that with the gene of such a kind, it is sharing economy, and vice versa (Table 2.1).

C2C Mode

C2C Mode is the most typical and common pattern, where both suppliers and demanders are individuals and they trade on the socialized network platforms. Its core feature is that the connection and sharing between suppliers and demanders are completed directly on platforms through a series of procedures: registration, sourcing, order placement, service delivery, evaluation and sharing, after-sales service. In the whole process,

M. Huateng et al., *The Chinese Sharing Economy*,
https://doi.org/10.1007/978-981-33-6494-3_2

Table 2.1 Four business models

		Demander	
		Customer	*Business*
Supplier	Business	B2C Mode	B2B Mode
	Customer	C2C Mode	C2B Mode

platforms are only playing the role of matching supply and demand information.

According to statistics from Tencent Research Institute, the C2C business model was the main trading pattern in over 80% of more than 35 areas of sharing economy in 2015, suggesting that the individual participation-focused pattern is the mainstay of sharing economy.

C2B Mode

Suppliers are individuals, while demanders enterprises. Both parties trade through specialized sharing platforms. Its core feature is the same as that of C2C mode, that is, the connection and sharing between suppliers and demanders are completed directly on platforms, and platforms are only playing the role of matching supply and demand information. Yet, its biggest difference from that of C2C mode is that its demanders are enterprise users.

C2B model may be one of the development trends of sharing economy. At the Executive Meeting of the State Council on January 27, 2016, Premier Li Keqiang pointed out that C2B is the trend of the times. In the C2B context, enterprises will be no longer isolated firms but the ones which are closely connected with markets through the internet and communicate flexibly with consumers at any time. Being a new business model in the Internet era, the C2B model will hold an increasingly important position in sharing economy and it will eventually grow into the decisive force in shaping the business landscape in the future.[1]

[1] Additional Readings: http://news.xinhuanet.com/politics/2016-01/31/c_128688663.htm.

B2B Mode

B2B mode means sharing of idle resources between enterprises through sharing platforms, which play the role of supply and demand matching. For example, sharing of idle production devices, and its typical entity is Floow2. Another case in point is sharing unused medical equipment, and its typical entity is Cohealo.

Although C2C is the main model of sharing economy for the moment, we believe that B2B mode will be its prospect, and enables enterprises to provide these resources beyond individuals' capabilities. We anticipate that the B2B model will also have a role to play in the sharing economy.

B2C Mode

Like B2B, B2C also counts enterprises as its suppliers and come in two variants:

One of the two variants is that suppliers are enterprises with idle physical resources, demanders individuals, and socialized network platforms the managers of idle resources taken in from suppliers, directly connecting demanders in the capacity of independent contractors and earning price differences on their deals with the demanders. The representative enterprises include YOU+ and WeWork, which take in idle spaces, decorate them, and then rent them out to customers. In a sense, the suppliers in such a model are similar to intermediaries. A case in point is Zipcar.

The other is the sharing by enterprises of its idle resources to individuals via socialized network platforms, which are responsible for matching information and charging management fees thereon. For example, Didi Bus and travel or leasing firms with idle buses provide bus services to individual users through the Didi platform.

The B2C mode represented by Zipcar was the dominant pattern in the earlier days of sharing economy, but the C2C mode featuring decentralization, light-assets, and low-costs has gained traction over time. The future trend will be the coexistence of C2B and B2B modes. Whatsoever its name, the core purpose is to share idle resources and reduce costs rather than to widen the price differences for profit.

Given no authoritative definition of sharing economy, many issues remain open to academic debates. Some scholars, for example, hold that sharing economy doesn't always come with the conditions for seeking profits. Take Juliet Schor as an example. In her paper: *Debating the*

Sharing Economy, she classifies sharing economy platforms into two groups: for-profit and non-profit instead of maintaining that sharing economy must be for-profit.

She holds that such sharing platforms that are run for purpose of non-profit public welfare in essence function as "public goods". Many public goods have a G2P (government-to-peer or government-to-individual) structure rather than a P2P structure.

Some scholars and institutions claim that since sharing economy is known as an activity between individuals, B2C mode should fall into the category of sharing economy, but others disagree.

Ms. Benita Matofusca, Founder of The People Who Share, contends that agents in sharing economy are either individuals or organizations. Thomas Spanda, a British scholar and media celebrity, agrees with her view and says in his article titled *C2C is Prelude to B2B in Sharing Economy* that sometime in the future, resource sharing between entities will demonstrate great potentials for development, and sharing such high-value resources as heavy equipment will bring huge incomes to enterprises. He further claims that sharing economy isn't exclusively limited to sharing among individuals, and sharing of high-value resources among businesses will rise to be the mainstay in sharing economy.

CHAPTER 3

Issues of Economic Surplus to Be Solved

Economic Surplus Changes Everything

In 2015, we thought about such a question: Now that tourism economy, roughly, is how much we spend on travel or tourism around the world, Golden Week economy refers to our consumption within a 7-day-long public holiday in May each year, and then, how should we understand sharing economy from the perspective of economics?

Later, we hit upon a phrase: economic surplus, and thus found the key to answering the question. We believe that sharing economy is an effective approach to stimulate economic benefits by massively activating economic surplus and can be able to address the issue of economic surplus.

The so-called economic surplus is the product of socialized mass production and socialized excessive consumption. In the period of agricultural society, social production was insufficient, and human beings tried to increase production by employing agricultural animals, and social demand remained unable to be fully met. In the industrial age, machines were used, and productivity was greatly increased, but social demand was often weak due to over-consumption in many fields, resulting in an oversupply of goods. For example, in the early 1980s, Television sets were in short supply. To get one, you had to wait in line. Yet, when you already had two or three TVs in your house, did you still have a reason to get additional ones? But makers kept on churning out them, and therefore there was an excessive inventory. Some manufacturers might claim that there was no excessive inventory at our factory. But the fact is that a

M. Huateng et al., *The Chinese Sharing Economy*,
https://doi.org/10.1007/978-981-33-6494-3_3

considerable part of their products would never land in the hands of end-users. They had to be stored in the warehouses of various distributors. As socialized mass production develops and consumers are richer, shopping is no longer a necessity but a habit, that is, you buy as long as you like to. Therefore, many goods end up prematurely in dustbins. Such a phenomenon is the consumer surplus.

At the enterprise level, economic surplus comes in the form of idle inventory and capacity while at the individual level, it comes in the form of idle funds, idle goods, and cognitive surplus, which are commonly known to us as spare money, goods, and time.

In the past, economic surplus, like glass fragments, scattered here and there in various quarters across our society. Their integration cost was extremely high, and it was also difficult to bring out their social benefits. So their sharing was simply done in a limited scope, if any.

Nowadays, things are different. Thanks to the internet technologies, numerous glass fragments scattered here and there are pooled and pieced together on specialized platforms to match supply and demand across the whole society and generate new economic benefits - forming new glass mirrors.

In piecing together fragments into mirrors, sharing economy solves the issue of economic surplus. This might be as well-known as the "mirror effect".

This can be summed up in four sentences:

1. Any surplus can be shared;
2. Where there are individuals, there is a surplus;
3. Any sharing can be achieved; and
4. Any sharing benefits all sharers.

The first sentence means sharing economy was originated from economic surplus. Economic surplus, as mentioned above, comes at the individual level in the form of three idle resources: spare things, spare money, and spare time, and at the enterprise level idle inventory and capacity. As long as there is an economic surplus, there will be sharing behavior.

The second sentence points out that where the economic surplus is. Economic surplus begins with individuals, enterprises, governments, cities... As long as there are individuals, there must be an economic surplus.

The third sentence says that the network platform supports the development of sharing economy. The sharing of the economic surplus is not equal to sharing economy. The sharing of sporadic, scattered and fragmented glass bits must be done to a critical mass to be sharing economy. Just as networks are necessary to connect all individuals, so is advanced network platforms to connect economic surplus. Almost all imaginable contents can be realized on the internet platforms. Of course, such sharing should be disintermediated.

The fourth sentence means that sharing economy is sure to generate benefits. The fundamental purpose of individuals' participation in sharing economy is to cut down costs and benefit both parties: demanders get reduced costs in getting what they want while suppliers get additional incomes from what they provide. Otherwise, if a sharing economy platform fails to create a win-win dynamic for both suppliers and demanders, it will be doubtful.

From another point of view, that is, from the perspective of production and consumption or economic surplus, let's have a look that what issue can be solved.

Newspapers and television have said that nowadays, we are in a bad economic situation and an important factor behind the current global economic downturn may be over-consumption, which can lead to serious social problems. For example, the over-consumption of cars results in traffic jams and encroachment on sidewalks in urban areas and housing over-consumption, where people have more houses than they need for living in, enables housing to be a speculative demand and its prices to rise constantly. As a result, ghost towns have cropped up in the country and the national economy has been held hostage.

From the perspective of sharing economy, how should we solve the issue of over-consumption? The solution is to enhance the utilization of surplus resources. Due to the consumers' over-consumption, they gather too many unwanted goods in their hands, which can be re-circulated and re-used for meeting the needs of life without additional production.

In addition, is the sharing economy thinking also helpful in mitigating over-production? It is also a rather tricky reality. Overproduction leads to a huge overstock. Besides price reduction, is there any other option to destock? In theory, leasing as an alternative to selling may help cut down the stock. With too many unsold houses on hand, real estate developers resort to renting them out to reduce their inventories and get back the tied-up funds; and automakers also rent out their newly-built cars instead of selling them.

But sadly, the solution mentioned above doesn't work with excess milk production. The maker has to sell excess milk at reduced prices or dump it. Does sharing economy still work with milk surplus?

With various problems, a case-by-case approach should be adopted. But sadly, the solution mentioned above doesn't work with excess milk production. The maker has to sell excess milk at reduced prices or dump it. Does sharing economy still work with milk surplus?

With various problems, a case-by-case approach should be adopted. The reason why lease as the alternative to sale works with excess houses is that houses can be reused. Here, we separate the ownership of a house from its access (the right to use). With its ownership unchanged, we can rent the access. Being a fast-moving consumer goods, milk has a shorter consumption cycle and a higher rate of recurring consumption. A loss of its access is the loss of its ownership, so how can milk be leased to lease?

If there is a sharing economy platform for economic surplus, you will be in a completely different situation. We assume that this platform is open to large numbers of active users across the country, then, excess products in some regions may likely become the best-selling ones in other regions!

Surplus resources abound in the society; and due to the lower efficiency in supply-demand matching arising from information asymmetry, they stay idle for long. If there are platforms for coordinating supply and demand, these idle resources scattered across the society can be fully utilized and their values can be brought into full play.

The value of sharing economy lies in enabling surplus resource matching across the society. In the past, economic surpluses were scattered in a fragmented form across all quarters of the society, so their integration cost was extremely high and it was difficult to bring out their due social benefits. Nowadays, sharing economy provides an innovative solution to the issue of economic surplus: with mobile internet technologies, online payment platforms, convenient transportation and logistics networks, and strong social media tools, economic surpluses can be effectively and efficiently integrated on specialized platforms for matching supply and demand across the whole society, producing new economic benefits.

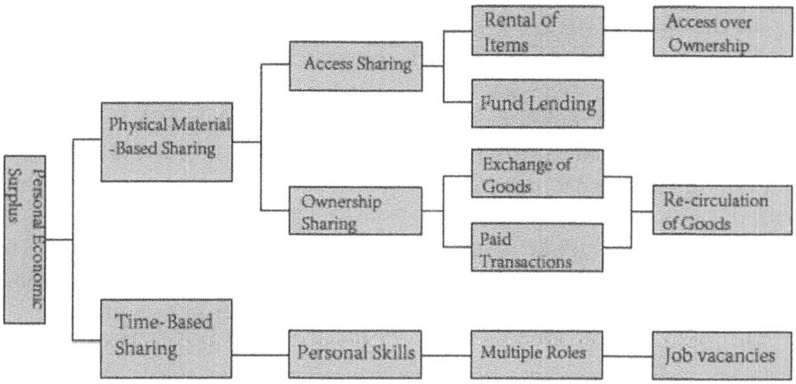

Fig. 3.1 Economic surplus sharing

Sharing Patterns for Three Types of Surplus

By the definition of economic surplus, we classify sharing behaviors into three patterns:

> The first pattern is the sharing of access surplus. The access goes before ownership;
> The second one is the sharing of time surplus. With multiple "roles", individuals can sign up for various job openings;
> The third one is the sharing of ownership surplus. Secondhand items can be recirculated, leading to various benefits, including environmental protection and resource efficiency (Fig. 3.1).

First Pattern: Sharing Success Surplus

The first pattern by which economic surplus is shared is excess access sharing. When having amassed your own items in excess of your need, you may as well rent them out. This is also the most popular way to share personal idle resources, and can roughly consist of 2 scenarios: idle items can be shared through online rental platforms, while idle funds mainly through P2P lending platforms by lending to third parties.

Online leasing has expanded rapidly in various sectors, such as travel, real estate, office space, and idle funds.

In the travel sector, a plethora of innovative modes of sharing economy have sprung up. Besides overseas entities such as Uber and Lyft and domestic ones like Didi Chuxing, there are a wide range of variants, including tailored taxi services for the high-end business car market segment, low-cost fast-ride services, private car-based taxi services, carpooling services for passengers traveling on the same routes, and online reserved bus services for multiple passengers along established routes.

This mode has rapidly gained traction and expanded into all segments of the sector. Apart from cars, it seems that any kind of means of transport can be shared, including ships, private jets, yachts, bicycles and so on.

Airbnb is a game-changer in the traditional hotel sector. Not only can ordinary individuals rent their own rooms at lower prices than hotels but also can flexibly choose rental schedules and tenants, without excessive constraints. Of course, the key here is that private homes to be to leased must stay idle. While the booming sharing economy has spawn "professional resources", including middleman landlords and professional landlords, but a large number of idle rooms are freed up to create new value, improving their efficiency of resource utilization.

From idle residential room rental for consumers to idle office space rental for freelancers and entrepreneurs, housing rental has further expanded both in scope. Owners of idle office spaces can directly connect with tenants via sharing platforms such as Ma3office.com. In addition, more entities share office spaces in the rental-decoration- sublease model of WeWork.

In terms of idle funds, most scholars hold that P2P lending and equity crowd-funding are innovative forms of sharing. Without bank intermediation, the point-to-point model enables individuals to complete financial transactions directly with others, having lower transaction costs for either investors or borrowers than these at financial institutions.

This is especially typical of crowd-funding transactions. With little access to bank loans in earlier stages, project owners have to raise funds through project financers. A web-based crowd-funding approach can reduce information asymmetries in financing and enhance market influence.

The appeal of these "lease economy" sharing platforms is that they can create a win-win situation for both parties to transactions. In theory, lessors earn incomes from their resources, and lessees have lower costs and higher convenience than at large professional organizations. Therefore, regardless of ages or enterprises, more and more consumers prefer to buy the use-value of a product rather than the product itself.

The concept of "access over ownership" eliminates the exclusive and competitive features of personal items, enabling personal items also to be shared among consumers in the person-to-person form. This is the first important form of sharing economy - sharing access surplus.

Second Pattern: Sharing Time Surplus

In addition to items, personal labor skills can also be shared as long as you have spare time. This practice is known as "gig economy" or "self-employment economy". This approach corresponds to a huge number of jobs created by online marketplaces, including a variety of payment errands and office chores.

A phrase: cognitive surplus was coined for this purpose by Clay Shirky. According to her, the cognitive surplus is a new resource that is created as the accumulated free time across the world increases. In addition, the two most important transformations that enable us to use this resource have already taken place - the free time of more than 1 trillion hours per year available to skilled persons around the world and the invention and proliferation of public media. With the two conditions in place, ordinary citizens can spend their free time on activities they like or care about.

Labor skill-sharing suggests that our understanding of human resources should be revolutionized.

In practice, sharing economy is not limited by entry barriers of industries, reduces employment thresholds, and releases tremendous production capacity with lower social costs. In the past, these productive capacities, scattered in various quarters of the society and tied up by solidified traditional management systems, could not be part of socialized mass production, such as tailored taxi service drivers, short term-rent homeowners, personal cooking service providers, independent couriers and so on. Sharing economy is an unprecedented revolution, quietly turning millions of people into part-time workers and creating a large number of jobs. As sharing economy further develops, will it remain necessary in the future for you to stick to a nine-to-five o'clock job as you do now?

Along with time surplus sharing comes a new social trend of "playing various roles". For example, although you're a doctor in profession, you may also be able to play other roles. Being skilled at tutoring, driving, cooking, and so on, you can be a teacher, driver, chef, or so on during your spare time. Which role and in which sector you play is up to your willingness and skills. There have already been such platforms over there! (For further information, see Chapter 16).

In the travel sector, online substitute driving service is also developing like a raging fire. In contrast to car sharing, substitute driving service sharing is sharing a driver's driving skills and spare time. Substitute driving service demand arises from an employer being unable to be behind the wheel personally. Via a substitute driving service App, you can employ the nearest driver for driving your car to a designated location on agreed fees for the service. Such service is needed mainly on the occasion when a car owner is in a drunken state and, to a lesser degree, on others like tourism, business trip, and long-distance travel.

In the catering sector, online employment comes mainly in the form of sharing cooking skills. By eliminating information asymmetry in the personal cooking skill market and tapping supply-side resources, some sharing platforms bring together these idle cooks ready to share their cooking skills to form a "personal cooking skill-sharing platform". These platforms may take various forms: for example, Huijiachifan (dinner-at-home), homely dish takeout services meeting recurring rigid demand; Mishi, an e-commercial platform exploring folk cuisines; Woyoufan (I offer featured foods), a Chinese answer to EatWith, which offers highly personalized packaged services by integrating a variety of elements: catering, social engagement and culture; and Aidachu (Skilled Chef), an on-site cooking service responding to fancy banquets. In sharing their personal cooking skills and spare time, cooks earn incomes and reap the sense of personal fulfillment, while diners have the opportunities to get a taste of a wide variety of featured cuisines.

Moreover, sharing economy also reshapes the domestic service sector. Care.com, a U.S. domestic service platform, reviews, and lists service demand information from individuals for response from potential domestic workers online. A significant part of respondents are part-time workers.

Due to reintegrating forces of individuals in a society, the marriage of sharing economy and education alleviates the imbalance between supply and demand in the sector. Each one may become a tutor by providing training services with his skills and knowledge, and can also become a student by signing up for training sessions. In addition, the marriage of sharing economy and education also mitigates the information asymmetry in the education industry. Demonstration and communication on sharing platforms enable instructors of all kinds, including individuals and institutions, to directly connect and engage with students, not only removing information barriers at traditional training institutions with lower transaction costs but also freeing increasing numbers of teachers from their traditional training institutions. Nowadays, either independently or in a team, many instructors give lectures on sharing platforms like Genshuixue. Another merit from the marriage of sharing economy and education, also the most creative part of sharing economy, is breaking down the clubs of "strong relationships" exclusive to experts and allowing the general public to get access to hotshots with "weak relationships".

Unlike knowledge sharing platforms, e.g. Zhihu, Baidu Knows, etc., knowledge sharing in the education industry is more focused on one-to-one services, and provides in-depth information services highly targeted to specific topics and needs from users. The cases in point include telephone/online communication services, such as Zhide and Bangyang, and one-to-one face-to-face chit-chat services, such as Zhaihang. Both models provide scenarios for targeted, private knowledge services and create possibilities for in-depth interpersonal engagements.

In the sharing economy era, professional service providers, like Witkey, have their brightest day. Witkey shares wisdom, knowledge, expertise, skills and so on with demanders through the internet, and gains tangible benefits, with most of its task undertakers being part-time workers, its focus mainly on cultural and creative industries, and its business scope covering various services, including architectural design, graphic design, advertising design and website development services.

Furthermore, there are also many sharing-oriented entities in the legal affairs and professional consulting sectors. For example, LVGOU, a legal services platform, rallies idle productive forces scattered across the society in the crowd-sourcing way to enable everyone to become an agent in corporation registration.

Another niche in the huge professional service market, the craft men or artisan segment, is increasingly popular, with traditional offline craftsmen in manicure, makeup, massage, and other areas being readier to share their skills. Being oriented to stock markets, sharing platforms in these niches alleviate the information asymmetry between supply and demand, improve the efficiency of information matching, and facilitate service scheduling for both users and craftsmen.

Online hiring has also spawned C2C task collaboration model, for example, TaskRabbit. Through platforms, users post their task demands to have others complete them, or publish their skills to provide services. C2C task collaboration model has gained rapid traction in various sectors, such as nursing, logistics, medical care and so on.

With the population aging quickly in China, the issue of socialized old-age care is coming up. More entities in China, including Peibama, are wading their way into home-based old-age care sector in sharing economy mode. Known as Health Managers, caregivers are mainly medics at community-based health care system and graduates in nursing, and pay visits to the elderly at their home according to service appointments, checking their needs and providing health services. Community doctors regularly provide the services, including "doing medical examination for the elderly at their homes" and "accompanying the elderly to see their doctors at community hospitals".

Another market is pet-care. With the increasing demand of traveling and returning home, traditional professional foster care entities cannot meet the needs of pet owners due to limitations in room, time and funds. With pet family foster care platforms such as Petbang and Rover, pet owners may have their pets taken care of by foster carers, and families with the luxury of taking care of pets can also be foster carers, offering foster care services to pet owners.

In the logistics, by combining with express delivery, sharing economy integrates mass idle capacities, and efficiently dispatch independent couriers or idle freight vehicles nearest to demanders via geographical location apps to pick up goods at the demanders and deliver them at the destinations. In the cases of intra-city logistics, it is much faster and more time-saving than traditional express delivery. There are many platforms of such collaborative logistics, including Rrkd.cn, Dada Distribution and Jingdong Crowdsourcing.

Innovative logistics modes of this kind will also be the development trend of remote distribution in future. In his article: *the Zero Marginal Cost Society*, Jeremy Rifkin predicts that traditional point-to-point and hub-and-spoke transportation lose ground to the distributed joint transportation with the increasing popularization of logistics internet. A driver transports goods from a production center to a destination, and then transports a new batch of goods to be delivered on his way back. The sharing economy pattern operates in this way: the first driver delivers the goods at a closer center where he picks up another batch of goods to be delivered on his way back, and a second driver is responsible for moving the goods delivered at the center by the first driver to the next center, which may be a port, a railway freight yard or an airport, till the goods are relayed by various drivers along the whole transportation route to the destination.

Third Pattern: Sharing Ownership Surplus

Many people may not realize that the transfer of ownership will also become an emerging game of disposing of economic surplus as many kinds of idle resources can be thrown back into the circulation cycle. A typical approach is secondary trading.

Online secondhand item trading, to be exact, refers to transactions of secondhand item ownership between individuals through socialized network platforms, namely secondhand item trading in short. By sending secondhand items staying idle into the circulation cycle and putting them into use once again, we improve their utilization rates. In contrast to the first pattern, secondhand item trading is based on the sharing of their access and ownership.

There are two contributing factors to the popularity of secondhand item trading.

One is the excitement of online shopping, which leads to impulse shopping and excessive consumption. Over recent years, the price war in online shopping has been the handiest tool by major e-commerce platforms. Various eye-catching promotion stunts, such as discounts, flash sales and sales with freebies, reduce the prices of goods far below their original prices, stimulating the buying impulse of consumers: just buy it regardless of their need. For example, during the Double Eleven (Nov. 11) Shopping Festival in 2015, Alibaba garnered the sales revenue of RMB 91.217 billion, up 59.7% over RMB 5.71 billion in 2014.

Most of the buys from impulsive online shopping end up as "immovable" items staying idle long at home, for example, rarely-worn new clothes, unpractical fancy housewares, and luxury goods heavy in psychological value but light in practical function. These buys soon become wastes upon being bought, not only suffering a sharp drop in value but also being a great drain on household space.

With a large population, China has a huge advantage in resource sharing and migration. The booming online shopping has spawn a large number of "shopaholics", who can't restrain from buying online and regret over their excessive buying afterwards, and the result is a large number of idle items over there. Hence, China has a very large potential second-hand item market.

By trading idle items in the secondary trading, sellers can not only recover part of costs for funding new purchase demands, but also making room for new items in the next online shopping festival. It is really a more pleasant consumption spree. There is also a benefit for buyers: getting good quality goods at a lower price, namely the desirable cost-effectiveness. Thus, idle item trading platform is booming. According to industry insiders, there is always a peak of daily active users following shopping sprees.

The other is the quicker pace of product upgradation, especially digital devices. According to a 58.com survey: *Can Idle Items Turn into Money - Have You Ever Sold Secondhand Items Online?*, 72.12% of responders choose digital products, such as mobile phones, computers, cameras and so on. Deloitte Touche Consulting's analysis shows that out of 1.4 billion smart phones sold globally in 2015, 1.0 billion were done for trading-up. About 70% of smart phone users in 14 developed markets upgraded their phones in the past year and a half.

Therefore, as idle items piles up, online secondhand item trading platforms in the secondhand item trading market, including Xianyu, Zhuanzhuan, and Youxian, see their business booming.

Secondhand items are traded in various forms: barter, purchase or anything between the two. Sometimes, transactions occur in a weak relationship between strangers, while on the other, in a strong relationship between contacts in social networks.

The first form is barter.

The typical cases are transactions on the secondhand item sharing platform: Yerdle. Individuals log in the site Yerdle through their social accounts, and share their idle items between friends free of all charges except for the freight fees. Yerdle platform has 12,000 registered users, and a quarter of them browse the platform every week to check for desirable things.

The startup is among the pacesetters for collective consumption. Those believers of sharing economy hold that products made of compressed raw materials are more environmentally friendly, and thus is a more important approach to drive up their utilization rates.

The second is paid transactions, which can be done in two ways: C2C mode and C2B2C mode.

The typical case of C2C mode is Zhuanzhuan. The idle item transfer App developed by 58 Fair and Tencent is committed to freeing up the pent-up demands in second-hand item market from mobile device users. According to statistics, the platform attracted over 100,000 registered users on its launch day, over 5000 new listings were posted each day within the first week, and thousands of transactions a day now are completed on it.

Ali is planning to reshape Taobao's idle items trading community Xianyu into an independent business unit. The plan has invited keen interest from heavyweight CV/PE funds, such as Sequoia China and IDG Capital, and raised its market valuation over USD 3 billion. According to official data from Xianyu, the platform sees more than 200,000 idle items change hands a day.

CHAPTER 4

On-Demand Comes on the Heels of Sharing

The important article: *Workers on Tap* in the Economist in January 2015 briefed on a late phenomenon: employees can act like tap water, coming and going on demand and without being present in front of their bosses every day. It opens up a new domain (on-demand economy) for sharing economy from the "on-demand" perspective.

The article claims that on-demand economy is rising in such places as San Francisco and New York, where young technicians at big companies, including Google and Facebook, appoint Handy or Homejoy for cleaning up apartments via applications on their mobile phones, buying and delivering foods via Instacart, washing clothes by Washio, and purchasing flowers by BloomThat, etc.

The developers of these apps draw their inspirations from the ride-hailing app Uber.

The article analyses that knowledge-intensive companies have outsourced an increasing part of their work so as to cut costs and enable smarter full-time employees to focus on more productive work.

Given a growing number of such companies, the article points out that this boom marks a new phase of deeper transformation for sharing economy. Nowadays, delivering labor and services via ubiquitous smartphone platforms in a variety of new ways will challenge many of the basic theories of the twentieth century, including the nature of companies and career structures.

M. Huateng et al., *The Chinese Sharing Economy*,
https://doi.org/10.1007/978-981-33-6494-3_4

When it comes to on-demand economy, we, especially IT professionals, may recall the phrase: "on demand" put forward by IBM a decade ago. It was translated at the time into the Chinese expression "随需应变" instead of "应需", perhaps, for the purpose of being more impressive. In 2007, IBM unveiled a "new version": *E-Business, On Demand* (《电子商务, 随需应变》)—claiming that businesses could easily sort out, optimize and integrate the entire process within an enterprise from order placement to final products, and then thread together the entire supply chain through e-commerce way, connecting their external key partners, suppliers and customers.

Today, on-demand economy is all the rage. At this point, a question pops up: are on-demand economy and sharing economy the same thing?

A specialist website The On-demand Economy defines on-demand economy as a collection of business solutions to making everyday life easier and more efficient. This collection and its participants are reshaping the consumer experience over the last decade and setting the trend in the world. By the definition alone, it seems that on-demand economy has nothing to do with sharing.

However, a closer look into its links, we find something surprising.

The site breaks down on-demand economy companies by business type into various groups: business services, express delivery, education, in-home care, health & beauty, domestic service, P2P products, parking, pet care, booking & ticketing, transportation and travel, etc.

This classification is very similar to ours of sharing economy. We can also find that most of the enterprises in each category on the website are exactly the ones in sharing economy, including Uber, Airbnb, TaskRabbit, Postmates, etc.

On-demand economy more focuses on the rental and sale of idle items and spare time. For example, in their paper: *How On-demand Economy is Changing Workers' Compensation*, Denise Johnson and Andrew Simpson comment, based on Dr.Robert Hartwig's ideas, that on-demand economy, including temporary drivers, labors, landlords and independent professionals are transforming the U.S. labor and insurance industries.

Uber Founder Travis Kalanick said he preferred to define sharing economy as "on-demand economy". In his opinion, Uber enables passengers to get car-hailing at any time as they like. Uber is also the embodiment of on-demand economy for drivers. Drivers are working from the very moment they activate the app, and getting off duty from the very moment they deactivate it. Just for the moment, few jobs can be started and stopped at any time the workers want to do so. Uber can serve consumers while allowing its partners to have a flexible work schedule.

The End of the Industrial Production Mode

On-demand economy heralds the advent of a new form of economic cooperation beyond Taylor's imagination and the end of the industrial age. The master in management and founder of the scientific management theory system in the early twentieth century said in his book: *the Principles of Scientific Management* that just as a machine can save labor, scientific management is supposed to increase the unit labor output. It has been described that in a Taylor-style factory, there is no one extra worker, and every worker is working like a running machine. Another guru Mr. Ford employed scientific management in the workshop to the extreme extent, and the standardized assembly line he invented is typical of the organization form of mass industrial production, representing the highest level of traditional machine-based mass industrial production.

They had never thought of the day when workers can no longer belong in their assembly lines or their factories.

On-demand economy put an end to the organizational form of the industrial society and its replacements have already shown up: the first is on-demand supply where all products and services can be gotten on demand; and the second is the different career pattern where all jobs can be temporary. On-demand economy links independent and free professionals with the masses, providing personalized services on a large scale.

In this new era, we are having a comprehensive psychological revolution in regarding jobs, workmates and employers.

Sharism

In short, sharing economy is a business in which you share your spare items, funds and time through websites, and get gains therefrom. If sharing economy is simply a "cool" business, how could it be so popular around the world, not only with the masses but also many governments? How could it invite so intensive research interest from many scholars? Is there really no consensus at all around the globe? Why are so many companies, not just in services and even in manufacturing, having a shot at the business modes of sharing or even "rent-over -sale"? There are, for sure, underlying causes of its popularity and boom.

Basic Ideas of Sharing Economy

One important idea of sharing economy is "having the right to us not the right to own" put forward by Airbnb Founder Brian Chesky. In the past, if I had a demand for a resource or an item, I bought it and had it completely. When we didn't need it later, the resource or item usually stayed idle for the rest of its life cycle. That is to say, we paid unnecessary extra expenses for a temporary need.

In sharing economy, we only pursue the use value of resources, not the resources themselves. That is, we only want to have the right of using them rather than owning them. This idea emphasizes the sharing of the right of using something without affecting owning it. For example, renting extra rooms, sharing your driving skills and your car, sharing a video clip, or sharing a text. As long as our needs can be met, it is not always necessary for us to obtain the ownership by buying them. Instead, we can rent or borrow them.

Another idea of sharing economy is "Enough is Best". In his best-selling book: *The Age of Sharing Economy*, Rachel·Botsman emphasized this idea. Sharing economy comes from some needs from human beings, including cooperation, sharing, personal choice, etc. Credit capital brings about the positive and favorable mass cooperative consumption, creating a new pattern of wealth and social value growth, and sharing economy disrupts some traditional consumption patterns. Rachel believes we're in such a period of change, and are waking up from hangovers of massive idleness and waste. Sharing economy can eliminate outdated business patterns, helping us overstep the wasteful pattern of overconsumption, teaching us what "Enough is Best" is.

In her bestseller: *The Mesh: Why the Future of Business Is Sharing*, Lisa·-Gansky integrates the two ideas into one, pointing out that the two key ideas sharing economy values are "Access over Ownership" and "Value Unused is Waste".

New Consumption Concepts

With the development of sharing economy, the new consumption concepts such as “Value Unused is Waste” and “Access over Ownership” have gradually shown up and taken root in our society. With less resources for the daily needs from more people, sharing economy provide conditions for more environment-friendly and sustainable development.

These new consumption concepts have stimulated the development of sharing economy, and the mainstream concept in the process of sharing economy development, in turn, has inspired the spread and influence of new consumption concepts.

In a society that values ownership, the holding of personal belongings is the symbol of an individual’s personal wealth and status, encouraging “excessive consumption”. In order to satisfy this desire, people keep on buying, using and phasing out products regardless whether or not they actually needed them, resulting in the piling-up of idle items. Having these idle items is a great waste for individuals and also excessive resource exploitation for the earth.

As the concept of sharing is deeply entrenched in our society, more people get used to the way of life of “light assets”. Instead of pursuing a complicated life, we cut off life from work, cast off trappings that generate no values and make the best of the surplus, thus contributing to environment protection and resource conservation. Sharing economy mitigates the overcapacity in the mass production pattern, cools down emulative consumption frenzies, fosters brand-new social supply models, and cultures the sustainable consumption concept of making the best use of things.

For example, nowadays, many young people have no longer taken car ownership as a status symbol and instead have more valued the freedom to travel. This consumption concept of paying for the use value of a product only rather than for the full ownership of it disrupts the thinking about private property rights in the traditional industry. Inspired by the new concept, more consumers turn to the way of “rent rather than buy and pay on demand”.

Driving Force Behind Social Development

To solve these puzzles, we may as well look at the dynamics behind sharing economy. There are at least two factors at work, with one being about the macroeconomic cycle, and the other about internet technology.

Sharing economy is not something new that came out of nowhere. From a macroeconomic perspective, being a product of the economic downturn cycle, and the 2008 financial crisis in the USA contributed to the rise of sharing economy.

New Century Financial Corporation, the second-largest subprime loan provider in the USA, went bankrupt in April 2007, triggering the subprime mortgage storm. Following the failure of Wall Street rescues, the disaster swept soon across the global financial system in 2008, making dents in all economies to varying degrees. For example, 760,000 jobs went away in the USA alone in 2008, sending the unemployment rate skyrocketing over 7% and well above the peak of 6.3% during the height of the 2003 downturn. According to statistic data released by Eurostat on October 31, 2008, the unemployment rate in the Eurozone was 7.5% in September, up from 7.3% in the same period in 2007.

However, we have a refrain since ancient times that while shutting the door on you, God, maybe, opens a window for you. Due to the continuing economic downturn, worsening employment, and reduced incomes amid the financial crisis, many individuals had to live on renting or selling their idle personal items, and many companies turned to share their office facilities to slashing business costs. A surprising finding was that sharing economy contributes to reducing spending (price is the primary consideration in participating in sharing economy) and earning extra incomes on idle assets. As a result, the concept of sharing economy has gained traction across the world.

The 2007–2013 period is admittedly the burgeoning phase of sharing economy. Airbnb, the iconic firm in short-term rentals, and Kickstar, the pacesetter in crowd-funding, were both born in 2008, Uber, the pioneer in ride-sharing, and TaskRabbit, the website for running-errand jobs, were both came into being in 2009, and Grubwithus, a food-sharing site, was founded in 2010. In particular, start-ups in the sharing economy grew by nearly 50% each year during the 2010–2013 period.

As we have seen, sharing economy spread in various areas, such as car and house rental, while the economic crisis swept across the world; and some sharing economy giants, including Airbnb and Uber, grew rapidly.

These developments reflected the need for cost and expenditure reduction amid the economic downturn in the USA, with many peoples having to do part-time jobs for extra incomes to make their ends meet and support their families. The plight has promoted the rapid development of sharing economy. So, we can say that the winter of the financial crisis objectively provided social conditions for the emergence and development of sharing economy.

The sharing economy had developed in China slightly slower until 2011, which was closely related to China's economic situation. Over recent years, China's economy has been shifting into a new normal, with its GDP having declined to 6.9% in 2015 since 2010, the 25-year low. The deepening economic downturn has reshaped the consumption concept of the general public, resulting in more and more consumers turning to the lifestyle of sharing economy. It was just during this period when most of the sharing economy enterprises in China came into being and grew.

In 2011, many online short-term rental platforms, including Tujia.com and Mayi.com, were started, Lufax, the top P2P lending website, was founded, and Chunyu.me, the iconic entity in domestic medical knowledge sharing, was founded. In 2012, the phenomenal enterprise, Didi, was established, and PP Car Rental, a P2P car rental platform, entered the market. In 2013, Rrkd.cn, the first-ever crowd-sourcing express service entity, was founded, and Edaixi.com, a crowdsourcing domestic service, was founded. In 2014, Didi's tailored taxi service was launched, many enterprises in carpooling and car rental were set up, personal cooking skill sharing entities, including Huijiachifan and Mishi, went into operation, various sharing patterns like Expertise Sharing and Office Space Sharing emerged, and the personal service Nishuowoban was launched. In 2015, Didi Hitch, Bus Service, and Substitute Driving Service were launched, various online shopping secondary trading apps, such as Taobao Xianyu, 58 Zhuanzhuan, and Jingdong Paipai were established, and sharing economy in a private kitchen, bus service, education, logistics, medical and other sectors continued to grow.

Another contributing factor is the new development that internet technology enables the connection between individuals.

One might wonder why the sharing economy failed to develop rapidly even with recurring economic crises in the USA before. Here, we have to mention another factor—the mobile Internet. It is the advent of smartphones that enabled connection among individuals: a process that functions like piecing together various glass fragments into a glass mirror and led to a booming sharing economy. So the credit for the rapid development of sharing economy should, first of all, go to the genius who invented an epochal product.

Except for the subprime mortgage crisis, the USA in 2007 was also marked by a revolutionary offering:—Apple Inc.'s smartphone iPhone. On January 9, 2007, Apple Inc. CEO Steve Jobs announced the arrival of the mobile Internet era at a global press conference, and on June 29, 2007, iPhone was launched.

Soon after, Google Inc. launched a massive promotional campaign on its Android Operating System. Under the initiative of Google, an open alliance of handset partners was established in November 2007, connecting 84 hardware manufacturers, software developers, and telecom operators in the industry. The alliance worked together to develop and improve the Android operating system. In October 2008, the first-ever Android OS-based smartphone was unveiled. Over the following years, the Android Operating System found its way into mobile phones, TV sets, cameras, game consoles, tablet computers, and other fields under the aggressive promotion of Google.

Mobile Internet cleared the way to every user. Thanks to efforts from Google and Apple, smart terminals also experienced explosive growth. Take Google as an example. According to the official data released by Google, Android overstepped Symbian in the first quarter of 2011 as the top operating system on the global market. In the fourth quarter of 2013, Android operation system-based phones garnered a 78.1% share of the global market: on September 24, 2013, there were 1.0 billion sets of Android operation system-based devices worldwide; and by September 2015, Android mobile operating system had 1.4 billion users.

The massive popularization of sharing economy across a whole society required unified information technology as the underlying foundation. Take the case of a car rental platform as an example. When a traveler sends a request through his mobile phone app, the car owner will receive a reminder, thus, the parties being connected and a transaction concluded. In the era without smartphones, you simply couldn't imagine such a scenario.

Besides mobile smartphone technology, sharing economy also relied upon various technologies, including big data and cloud computing, which make it possible to efficiently process massive amounts of information to realize the matching of supply and demands and provide conditions for massive commercial activities for individuals to randomly take part in.

Consider Didi Chuxing. On the strength of big data analysis, Didi improved the efficiency of its transportation capacity and other resources and developed to form an intelligent transportation ecosystem covering the whole country, with its taxi service available in 360 cities and 4 million orders fulfilled each day, its tailored taxi service available in 80 cities and 3 million orders fulfilled each day and its Hitch service available in 338 cities and 1.82 million orders fulfilled each day. Processing so many orders requires highly accurate data matching. To respond to surges in order, new big data analysis tools must be employed for analyzing drivers' working habits and assigning car-hailing orders in a targeted manner so as to get a higher matching rate, and for adjusting price rates in a real-time way to adapt to the rise and fall of service demand within a day so as to better meet the needs from consumers.

Uber uses big data technology to match the travel routes of various customers, eliminating the issue of information asymmetry between supply and demand. At the 2015 China International Big Data Conference, Jiang Tian, a big data expert at Uber China, cited "People Uber + ", demonstrated that the functional concept is to match travel routes of various travelers based on big data to adjust the balance of supply and demand in time. For example, after a passenger activates his car-hailing App for service, a car would arrive soon in five minutes. Once the passenger sits into the car, the back-end algorithm would find the next passenger being closest to the route for the car, making him having an efficient and convenient trip.

Also, another technology is playing a crucial role in this process: smart payments. While mobile Internet is the technical support for the development of sharing economy, then the wide commercial use of online payment, which knows no location and time constraints, is the guarantee to its massive development.

On the one hand, online payment can guarantee the property security for both suppliers and demanders. For example, room rent paid in advance goes into the escrow account of the platform, and it won't be released to the house owner once after the transaction is completed. Similar to the role of Alipay between buyers and sellers on the Taobao platform, online payment can promote the security and reliability in transactions. On the other, the convenience of online payment also provides a guarantee for efficient sharing. For example, Didi's enterprise payment service makes account settlements between various enterprises. When a user uses the enterprise travel service option, he needn't pay for the service out of his pocket and then gets a reimbursement later back at his company. His expenses are automatically charged into the enterprise account of his company. In most transactions, a physical meeting between sellers and buyers is unnecessary, as a result, the effective use of online payment platforms can increase the appeal to buyers and sellers.

In addition, precise location technology and map navigation technology, to name just a few, also play their roles in promoting the development of sharing economy.

One Hypothesis

The sharing economy draws its supercharged power from its Internet gene, not only delivering tremendous commercial practice values but also carrying extremely far-reaching social implications.

Sharing economy leads to an on-demand economy, and further then, to the individualized-need-based mass sharing.

The future society may be built on the individualized-need-based mass sharing, also commonly known as Sharism.

Sharism, in fact, is not far away from us. It is just around the corner for us and the whole society. To embrace sharism, we just need to take a small step forward in our business practice.

PART II

China: Dragon Is Seen in the Fields

CHAPTER 5

Current Status and Problems of Sharing Economy

Sharing economy has developed rapidly across the world, becoming an emerging driver of global growth in the post-financial crisis age. Relying on innovation platforms, it can match supply and demand in surplus resources with lower costs and at higher efficiency, and achieve the successful effect that "Every talent is given full play to and everything is made the best of". According to some preliminary statistics, the global trading scale of sharing economy in 2015 was about USD 810 billion. The sharing economy in China is on the rise, and has made remarkable innovation achievements in the fields of leasing, travel, and so on. Even the Communique of the Fifth Plenary Session of the 18th CPC Central Committee also proposed to develop sharing economy. Yet, in the process of developing sharing economy, we still have many problems to be solved, which deserve our attention.

Sharing Economy: Provide New Driving Forces for Innovative Economic Development

With the development of science and technology and the rapid increase of productivity and social wealth, economic surplus has become a new global problem. Economic surplus has brought about economic surplus resources, which come in the form of idle inventory and capacity at the enterprise level and of spare funds, goods, and cognitive surplus at the individual level. The sharing economy can release new economic benefits

M. Huateng et al., *The Chinese Sharing Economy*,
https://doi.org/10.1007/978-981-33-6494-3_5

by massively activating economic surplus. As Chinese Premier Li Keqiang put it at the 2015 Summer Davos Forum, sharing economy is a new approach to drive economic growth. Entrepreneurship and innovation through sharing and collaboration will come with lower thresholds, lower costs, and faster pace, contributing to carving out new development fields in China's sharing economy and enabling more people to participate in it.

Nowadays, China's sharing economy has achieved impressive results in many fields. In the field of idle real estate, some websites have promoted the development of the tourism economy by sharing on a rental basis. In the field of labor service, the online service crowdsourcing model has been accepted by the general public, creating millions of jobs and greatly easing the employment pressure. In the field of transportation, Didi Hitch transported 810,000 passengers back home before the Spring Festival holidays, alleviating the problem of insufficient transport capacity during the Spring Festival holidays to some extent and also demonstrating the huge adaptability of sharing economy to social problems. In addition, in the manufacturing sector, sharing economy is also spurring production innovations, with lots of innovative practices, such as shared supply chains and destocking on a rental basis, springing up.

Currently, the sharing economy in China is expanding beyond transportation and accommodation to many fields of personal consumption, and the enterprise-end market is gradually taking shape. With the development of sharing economy, the new consumption concept of "Value Unused is Waste, Access is Over Ownership" has become increasingly prevalent, and less resource consumption for the daily needs of more people provides conditions for green and sustainable development. It is foreseeable that the sharing economy trend, which has affected hundreds of millions of people, will provide a strong new driving force behind China's economic growth and push China's economy to shift into a new set of drivers of growth, turning service industry into the "main engine" of economic growth.

Constraints to the Development of Sharing Economy

Currently, China's sharing economy is still in the early stage of development, having an imperfect market. In 2015, the total scale of sharing economy in China exceeded RMB 1 trillion (less than 1.6% of its GDP, and the non-financial sharing economy accounted for less than 10%). In contrast, the total scale of sharing economy in the USA exceeded RMB 3 trillion (3% of its GDP, and the non-financial sharing economy accounted for more than 90%). So, China's sharing economy still has a long way to go. At present, there are mainly the following constraints:

1. **The management concept of supervising traditional industries is not helpful in industry innovation in the context of sharing economy.**

China's existing regulatory thinking is centered mainly on access to various market segments, and regulation is executed mainly by issuing licenses. In the era of sharing economy, there are a large number of cross-industry business areas, rendering the traditional segmented management model incapable of action. Putting the existing regulatory model into application mechanically would not only lead to a much lower regulatory effect but also do more harm than help to the emerging business forms. On the other hand, in the supervision of sharing economy, the practice of "pan-safety" is also an open question. Safety often is an important reason in dismissing a new business model in sharing economy. Yet, when it comes to safety, the debate does, more often than not, miss the point and unjustified by sufficient concrete arguments.

2. **The credit system and supporting institutions are to be improved.**

Credit is the "hard currency" in the context of sharing economy. Without mutual trust between suppliers and demanders, sharing and transaction can't take place. In sharing economy, a series of institutions, including second-generation ID card information verification, social account login, friendly relationship prompt, mutual evaluation system, personal profile, and insurance claims, are needed to rapidly enhance the credit relationship between economic participants. However, the credit system in China is still not perfect. For example, platforms can't get access to more authoritative credit information reports, such as issued by the Credit Information Center of the People's Bank of China and various administrative authorities (including public security organs, associations of industry and commerce businesses, taxation agencies, customs, etc.), and can only evaluate the creditworthiness of suppliers based on commercial credit reports and public comments, leaving some hidden risks or loopholes unidentified while creditworthiness examination of economic participants and the safety of sharing economy greatly curtailed.

3. **Insufficient infrastructure limits wide social participation.**

Sharing economy is a product of highly developed Internet, and its demand is discretely distributed in extensive urban and rural areas across the country. However, China's network infrastructure needs to be further improved. First of all, despite a 50.3% internet penetration rate, China still lags way far behind developed countries, where the penetration rates are more than 80%. Secondly, mobile broadband 4G/3G applications are mainly in economically developed regions, and sparsely in 3/4-tier cities and rural areas. Finally, the Internet tariffs are still too high, there is room for further reduction. Inadequate infrastructure capacity directly affects the participation of 1.3 billion people in the sharing economy.

Suggestions on Promoting Sharing Economy Development in China

1. **Public awareness: to further popularize the concept and value of sharing economy and improve the sharing economy data statistics mechanism.**

Starting with social awareness campaigns, school education and establishment of sharing economy demonstration cities, etc., the government may as well launch various publicity events on sharing economy to tout its positive effects on our society, economy, and environment, encourage students to participate in entrepreneurial and innovation projects of sharing economy, and dispel suspicions and misunderstanding of sharing economy so as to enhance the understanding of sharing economy and participation enthusiasm of the general public. In addition, the economic increment data from sharing economy is absent from the GDP statistics, so new data collection mechanisms should be established to effectively factor in the real impact of sharing economy on GDP and consumer price indexes, so as to provide accurate data analysis for the government's decision-making.

2. **Government regulation: to exercise inclusive governance and foster an open and inclusive regulatory environment.**

Nowadays, countries around the world attach great importance to developing the sharing economy, and many governments even have worked out related policies to promote the development of sharing economy. For example, the British government formulated the sharing economy plan in 2014, striving to build itself into a global center of sharing economy. The South Korean government is also deregulating the market, and it has proposed to build a "demonstration city" of sharing economy. As for new business forms and models in sharing economy, which are different from traditional ones, any impractical approaches to force new developments to fit with outdated frameworks will backfire. Therefore, regulators should adapt their regulation tactics to local realities on a case-by-case basis, timely revising or removing unreasonable rules and regulations to promote the development of sharing economy.

3. **Supporting institutions: to modify and improve the credit system and supporting institutions.**

First of all, we should vigorously develop the credit market, build up the social credit system, promote the seamless connectivity of credit information platforms, and dismantle information silos. We should also enhance the online disclosure and sharing of information resources such as credit records, early warning of risks and illegal and dishonest behaviors, and provide operators with services, such as credit information inquiry and online identity authentication. Secondly, we should further improve the social security and welfare mechanisms. Necessary insurance and benefits should be provided to sharing economy participants, and sharing economy employment guidance should be given to help job seekers increase their experience, skills, and incomes. Finally, sharing economy platforms should be encouraged to cooperate with insurance institutions to set up compensation funds or provide insurance products.

4. **Basic infrastructure: to quickly put in place necessary infrastructure facilities for sharing economy.**

We should further strengthen broadband infrastructure, increase internet connection speeds, reduce internet tariffs, and bridge digital gaps to enable more people to step into the floor of sharing economy and participate in sharing economy services. We should pioneer in building sharing economy demonstration cities to deliver a demonstration effect. And we should integrate sharing economy into government procurement to encourage institutions at all levels to use sharing economy platforms for procurement, transportation, accommodation, and other services.

CHAPTER 6

Urban Travel Sharing

Looking from the rest of the world, you will find that sharing economy practices in other parts of the world are more or less reflected in China, while looking from China, you will find that the grass of sharing economy in China is even greener. As a result, the authors sum it up with a Chinese ancient sentence: The Dragon is Seen in the Fields.

Looking up eastward around the 2nd day of the 2nd lunar month each year, you will see the brightest star Spica in the Black Dragon Constellation rising in the evening sky, the first time in a year that this constellation rises and shines upon the sunset. The marvelous spectacle is described as "Dragon is Seen in the Fields" in *The Book of Changes* and the "Dragon Raises its Head" in Chinese folk tales. A line to the spectacle below the *No. 9-2 Qian Diagram* in *The Book of Changes* goes: "龙见于野,利见大人", meaning that since the dragon is seen in the fields, it is the right moment for high-fliers to seek their aspirational goal, like starting a business.

The sharing economy is rising like a dragon on the horizon. From the perspective of industrial development, the sentence "Dragon is Seen in the Fields" is a perfect reflection of sharing economy in China. It's a sign that spring is in the air, and the golden moment is here for life to revive! Data shows that many areas of sharing economy are absolutely vibrant with energy, with some budding, some thriving and some advancing by leaps and bounds.

M. Huateng et al., *The Chinese Sharing Economy*,
https://doi.org/10.1007/978-981-33-6494-3_6

For example, in the area of shared travel, the market is very large. According to the Didi, the total number of orders for the Didi Chuxing platform (taxi service, tailored taxi service, fast ride service, Didi hitch, substitute driving service, bus service, test-driving service and enterprise service) reached 1.43 billion in 2015, nearly twice the total number of taxi orders across the USA in 2015 (about 800 million, according to IBIS World and Statistic Brain statistics) and well more than the global cumulative number of 1.0 billion orders for Uber. However, this figure was only one company's data, and if you looked at the entire industry, the figure was estimated to be around 2.0 billion.

In the area of shared accommodation, the market has grown at an alarming rate of one hundred fold in four years. According to iResearch Consulting statistics, the online short-rent market in China accelerated in 2012, with a market of RMB 140 million in the same year, about RMB 800 million in 2013, RMB 3.8 billion in 2014, and RMB 10.5 billion in 2015. So the claim that this market will explode to RMB billions is not a tall talk, and data from two other institutes, Sootoo and EnfoDesk, also show that the online short-rent market exceeded the mark of RMB 10 billion in 2015.

China's P2P online lending market came in at RMB 27 billion in 2013, and it exploded to a staggering level of RMB 975 billion by 2015. P2P online lending and crowd-funding in the field of fund sharing not only developed to a large scale, but also showed a trend of rapid development. According to 01Caijing Research Institute, the network crowd-funding market was at RMB 15 billion in 2015, and the total market for P2P lending and network crowd-funding was RMB 990 billion in scale.

According to the user data of ZBJ.com, in the field of shared assignments, there were about 3.10 million free labors in China in 2015, and the online employment market was about RMB 23.45 billion in scale.

In the field of second-handed item sharing, according to the data of iResearch Consulting, the second-handed car market was about RMB 500 billion in scale in 2015, among which the online transaction scale was about RMB 10 billion. The second-handed household appliances market was RMB 100 billion in 2015, among which the online transaction scale was about RMB 2 billion. In addition, the secondary trading market of other items, such as home articles, books, and toys, was relatively small in scale. Therefore, the total size of online secondary trading was estimated to be about RMB 20 billion.

China's sharing economy is entering the golden period, the reasons are summarized as follows:

First, a huge market. China is home to the world's largest user base, providing a precondition in terms of mass participation for the development of sharing economy. According to the 37th issue of the *Statistical Report on Internet Development in China* released on 22 January 2016 by China Internet Network Information Center (CNNIC), as of December 2015, Internet users in China swelled to 688 million persons and the Internet penetration rate rose to 50.3%, up by 2.4% points year on year. Online mobile phone users swell to 620 million persons, 63.03 million persons more than that at the end of 2014, and the proportion of Internet users using mobile phones increased to 90.1%. As a result, the mobile phone is the primary device to stimulate the growth of Internet users and also an important tool to promote the development of sharing economy. According to Nielsen's 2013 global survey of willingness to participate in sharing, 94% of Chinese respondents would like to share with others, ranking first among all countries, showing the popularity of sharing economy in China.

Second, a vibrant venture investment climate. Sharing economy came in China about three years later than overseas. The first cohort of sharing economy businesses were started around 2011, and the number of new entities suddenly spiked in 2014. Sharing economy start-ups have been well received by venture capitalists, who are always ready to pour a lot of venture capital into these newcomers to back their innovations. By the end of 2015, there were at least 16 unicorns (start-ups with a valuation of more than USD 1.0 billion) in eight industries, and more than 30 would-be unicorns (start-ups with a valuation of more than RMB 1.0 billion), with a cumulative valuation of more than RMB 70 billion. Of course, we have also noticed that with the development cycle of the investment industry, the global investment boom was also on the wane. Although start-up financing in some fields set into winter, the financial ammunition stashed at global PE/VC institutions remains enough for fueling the development of sharing economy start-ups for another couple of years.

Third, a favorable public environment. The Chinese government attaches great importance to sharing economy. In 2015, the term

> "sharing economy" appeared in the report of the Fifth Plenary Session of the Eighteenth CPC Central Committee. Chinese Premier Li Keqiang also endorsed the role of sharing economy and he pointed out that the sharing economy that is now thriving on a global scale opens a new way to boosting economic growth. Entrepreneurship and innovation through sharing and collaboration lower the threshold and costs but increase the speed of doing business. Thus, the space will be opened up for developing sharing economy in China and it is possible to get a lot of people involved. During the 2016 CPPCC and NPC sessions, Chinese Premier Li Keqiang touched on the topic of sharing economy twice in his *Report on the Work of the Government*, stating that sharing economy is a new driving force for economic development and a new potential for entrepreneurship and innovation. The People's Daily also commented: the evolution of the expression about sharing economy from "developing sharing economy" first appearing in 2015 in the official literature of China's Central Government to "promoting the development of sharing economy" and "supporting the development of sharing economy" in the *2016 Report on the Work of the Government* obviously not only reflects the Chinese Central Government's emphasis on sharing economy but also highlights its firm position and a clear attitude on sharing economy.

With a huge market and strong backing from venture capital and government policies, we believe, from the perspective of industrial development, that sharing economy has entered a golden period in China.

Although the business practice of sharism has encountered some obstacles in certain fields and some fields are just starting out while others are still warming up, the trend can't be stopped in China that sharing economy is sweeping across the country and sharism practice is solving actual social problems.

Let's take a look at the future scenarios first.

Google is developing its fully autonomous cars, or Google Driverless Cars, which will be able to drive safely on the road without a driver. News reports said that as of June 2015, Google announced that the vehicle had traveled 1.6 million kilometers in testing, mainly in San Francisco, Austin and Texas. These cities will be the first to launch driverless services.

Competition in driverless car sector is also intensifying. Unlike ordinary cars, Google's unmanned cars have no steering wheels and brake systems and can successfully deliver customers to their destinations with one click. The cars are suitable for different needs in a variety of scenarios.

Despite certain policy restrictions on particular cars of such a kind, Google is still pushing ahead with its driverless car project. Its stubbornness, we speculate, is driven not so much by the need to satisfy consumers' addiction to driverless cars as by the inspiration of sharing economy. Such a speculation is not groundless. Since February 2015, Google has been developing a service that can be combined with driverless cars. If successful, Google could compete with Uber in the market. In contrast, Uber, and a number of automakers are also developing and testing the driverless technology.

Google's move is a clear signal to challenge such ride-sharing pioneers as Uber and Lyft as well as the traditional rental industry. With such internet giants as Google stepping into the fray, we believe that sharing economy will become livelier and more promising.

It is imaginable that in the future, all driverless cars in a city will be shared via a unified platform according to personal needs. Upon an appointment, a driverless car will appear in front of you. It must be a magnificent scene. By then, there will be no need to have a private car, and there will be no need to worry about the public car use reform.

Such a driverless city may come true in about 10 years later. Today, it's burgeoning out of ground in its place of birth, California, Google is trying to break through restrictions imposed by local governments.

Three Modes of Travel

By now and in the Chinese cities on the opposite side of the earth, we have not gotten ready to be driverless; and we even still have a mixed feeling of resistance, suspicion, and rejection towards a shared car ride.

We have long been used to going about relying on urban transportation, either private transportation, such as walking by foot, riding bicycles or motorcycles, driving private cars, etc., or public transportation, such as taking buses, subways, light rail trains, taxis, etc. Recently, there has emerged a third mode of travel, including online car sharing, online tailored taxi services, online P2P car rental. The three travel modes cooperate with and complement one another, thus improving urban transportation and travel systems. Especially, the third mode as a sharing economy form is shaping insensibly our lifestyles and also raising a lot of controversies. How do we think of such changes in our modes of travel sharing economy has brought about?

As known to all of us, the first mode of travel is entirely anchored on personal means. Under such a mode, all have the incentive to have their own cars - You drive your own car, and I drive my own car - thus, fueling the mentality of keeping-up-with-the-Jones and the car-buying frenzies. Such an unrestrained growth in car ownership results in excessive resource redundancy, one of the root causes of economic surplus.

The second one is mainly anchored on the government and a small number of enterprises. The market is cultivated through policy provisions and thus is tainted with a distinct hue of government regulation. However, with a swelling urban population, the private car holding is increasing rapidly, but the development of transportation infrastructure can't keep up the pace, and so we get into an awkward predicament: huge and still-growing unmet demands versus the relatively slow-growing supply. When demand grows into an elephant, supply is still an ant that has not grown up yet. How can an ant support an elephant? This is the market dilemma for sharing economy arising from outdated regulatory approaches.

The third mode relies on the masses to reorganize social resources through market and technical mechanisms. It is a holistic, systemic and scientific one that plays the role of the Savior in removing such social headaches as ""an ant can't support an elephant".

Let's take the traffic problems in Chinese cities as an example.

In a report, Roland Berger Strategy Consultants researched urban traffic issues in the four dimensions: quantity, efficiency, quality and consequences. We step into their shoes in our analysis.

First, Quantity: consumer travel demand cannot be effectively satisfied, which is evidenced by the serious under supply of transportation means during rush hours in the morning and the evening. Take Beijing's taxi market as an example. Over the past decade or so from since 2003, the urban population has exploded by more than 7 million residents, while the total number of taxis on road has stayed unchanged at 66,000. Demand for taxis in Beijing during morning rush hours is three times higher than supply, a serious imbalance between supply and demand.

Second, Efficiency: consumer travel efficiency is low, which is evidenced by two obvious phenomena: serious traffic jams and longer travel times. According to the Roland Berger Strategy Consultants' report, in the second quarter of 2014, the travel efficiency index in China's top 10 cities was as low as 50% (the travel efficiency index is

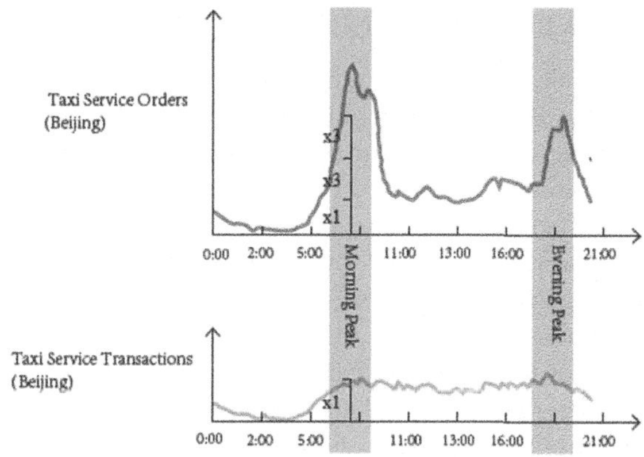

Fig. 6.1 Supply-demand relationship of taxi service market in Beijing during rush hours (*Source Comprehensive Urban Travel Reform in the Era of Mobile Internet*, Roland Berger Strategy Consultants)

measured by the ratio of the consumed time to a destination in a smooth situation against the actual time, and the closer the ratio to 100%, the more smooth the traffic is). A consumer in the top 10 cities loses on average 85 hours a year to traffic jams, with 100 hours lost for Beijing residents. Urban traffic congestion has risen among the most serious problems in China (Fig. 6.1).

Third, Quality: hierarchical demands in consumer travel can't be met, which is evidenced by scarce high-quality services. For example, special populations, including high-end businessmen, pregnant women, the elderly, children and patients, can't get access to personalized high-quality services, and taxis fail to provide a comfortable ride environment and quality service experience. According to the survey data from Roland Berger Strategy Consultants, 37% of urban residents claim that taxis cannot meet their upgraded travel demands.

Fourth, Consequences: unreasonable urban traffic planning has ended up with a lot of economic losses, serious environmental pollution and public security problems. According to statistics, about 600 million residents in 25 provinces suffered from smogs, and the number of air pollution days in Beijing hit 175 days in 2014. The primary pollution source of smogs is the excessive emission of motor vehicle exhausts from a large number of private cars on road.

Travel Sharing in the Third Mode

As known to us all, a crowd of antes can't support an elephant, not to speak of one ante. However, it would be a different picture should a city be full of antes. Yet, how can you fill your city with so many antes? The right solution is numerous private cars staying idle, that is, we have a high stockpile of idle social resources to be employed.

First of all, travel sharing is to solve effectively the issue of insufficient transportation capacities during rush hours by mobilizing idle vehicle resources to greatly increase the traffic supply through innovative business models. According to Roland Berger Strategy Consultants' statistics, the tailored taxi service market had nearly 300,000 taxis at the end of 2014, and the number of private cars ready for carpooling was more than 40 million.

Then, mobile car-rental and taxi-hailing platforms dramatically reduce the waiting and traveling times for consumers, thus reducing traffic congestion and improving travel efficiency. According to related research from Massachusetts Institute of Technology, carpooling can reduce traffic congestion by 55%. Besides, according to the Tsinghua Media Survey Lab's survey report: *2014 Mobile Travel White Paper*, with the rapid development of tailored taxi services in mobile travel service sector, 10 million private cars can be pulled off the road across the country in 2015, slashing the average daily congestion time in cities by 28.1% from 2014.

Further then, the car sharing service can effectively meet the multi-level, high-quality, and personalized needs for travel. For example, in contrast with others, Didi's tailored taxi service as a highly differentiated service catering to mid/high-end demands is more rigorous in the selection, training, and assessment of its drivers. Besides drinking water and a car charger, its cars are also equipped with anti-smog masks, Bluetooth headsets, on-board Wi-Fi for the convenience of consumers, and even seasickness bags are available for smokers. Pets are allowed to accompany their owners, and customized services are available for the elderly, the pregnant, and children.

Finally, travel sharing drastically slashes the waste of resources and energy, effectively reduces carbon emissions, and thus helps to protect the environment. The *Policy Recommendations on Promoting Online Tailored Taxi Services in China* by the National Institute of Financial Research at Tsinghua University asserted that car sharing contributes to reducing private car holdings, as proven by the fact of one more shared car for

4–10 fewer private cars in Europe, 6–23 fewer in North America, and 6–10 fewer in Australia, and significantly reduces the no-load operation mileage, as proven by the fact of one more car-sharing user for an average 28–45% less no-load operation mileage in Europe and 44% in North America. Further down the road, a drop in the no-load operation rate by 10% globally contributes to cutting down the carbon emissions by approximately 3.64 million tons, equivalent to the annual eco-compensation of 300 million trees.

According to Didi's big data, Didi contributes to reducing global annual carbon emissions by approximately 13.35 million tons, equivalent to the annual eco-compensation of 1.13 billion trees.

In fact, the third mode is efficient, easy to practice, and thus widely popular among consumers. Uber provides safe and low-cost tailored taxi services in 344 cities in 63 countries. Car sharing platforms like Didi Chuxing have fueled the frenzy of mass shared travel in China, with sharing travel forms and mobile application in the "Internet Plus Transportation" market, such as tailored taxi service, carpooling, periodical sharing, substitute driving and P2P car rental, springing up, being rapidly popularized and developed.

CHAPTER 7

Idle Housing Sharing

In October 2007, Joe Gebbia and Brian Chesky, two unknown college graduates, lived in a rented loft in San Francisco. A conference to be held there attracted many exhibitors and tourists, leading to an extreme short supply of hotel accommodation. The two students came across an idea: renting their living room in the loft to tourists for covering their rental for the loft. Acting without delay, Gebbia made the arrangement for the rental space: A few idle inflatable mattresses were laid out in the living room as the beds while Chesky log on to the local website to advertising their rental space. Everything went well. A couple of days later, three young people got living in their living room and the first fortune came into the pocket of the two grads. However, the tiny income alerted Brian and Gebbia that it is a nice business model. Now that so many guys have unoccupied rooms while so many outsiders wish to have the experience of living at home, why not launch a website to let everyone experience such a novel service?

So, Airbnb came into being in August 2008 and took hold in more than 34,000 cities globally by 2015, providing accommodation service worthy of more than 1.1 million rooms to users worldwide and posting 50,000 pieces of rental information. Within a short span of only seven years, Airbnb completed the process of its initial development and was cited by *The Times* as "eBay in Housing". In the summer of 2015, it garnered USD 1.0 billion in financing on a valuation of more than USD 24 billion and it is expected to reap a USD 3.0 billion EBIT by 2020.

M. Huateng et al., *The Chinese Sharing Economy*,
https://doi.org/10.1007/978-981-33-6494-3_7

Two Conditions for the Airbnb Model

The case shows that short-term rents like Airbnb are a new way to let out houses coming along with the rising sharing economy mode, and they thrive under two conditions: a booming tourism and a full-fledged online platform.

In China, there is no problem in meeting the first condition as tourism has boomed over recent years with more scenic spots developed. According to data from China National Tourism Administration, China saw its domestic tourism rise to 2.024 billion person-times in the first half of 2015, registering a 9.9% YoY increase; tourism-related consumption soar to RMB 1.65 trillion, up by 14.5% YoY and 4.1% points higher than the growth rate of the retail sales of consumer goods; and both hotel room revenues and the average guestroom price rate rise by approximately 1% on a recovering star-rated hotel business. Apart from tourism, business travel is also an important factor to promote the development of the short-term rent industry. Short-term rent saves travelers much in accommodation expenses, and thus is popular with companies.

The second condition is also no problem. In the context of sharing economy, more and more people are willing to rent their idle houses to users with short-term accommodation needs. With lower prices for service at the same level and a greater sense of belonging from the at-home atmosphere, short-term rent rooms deliver a different experience from traditional hotels. Furthermore, short-term rent rooms enjoy additional advantages over hotels in the room type option, the flexible lease way, and the service experience.

According to the data from United Nations' World Tourism Organization, Chinese tourists made 109 million outbound trips in 2014, catapulting China to be the biggest spender on tourism since 2012. To tap such a huge market, Airbnb adjusted its business strategy and served 700% more Chinese outbound tourists in the period of 2014–2015, signifying that China has become its fastest-growing market.

What are the implications for the real estate sector in China of the confluence of two conditions: a sizzling hot tourism and the emergence of housing short-term rent platforms, which have turbocharged Airbnb's global expansion?

The high stockpile of properties has become a drain on the Chinese economic growth. According to the data from China National Bureau of Statistics, as of October 2015, the growth rate of national real estate development investment has slid by nearly 90% in 20 consecutive statistical periods, with the inventory floor area near 700 million square meters. Worryingly, the figure only covers the unsold houses in completed projects, not factoring in the potentially-unsold houses in the pipelines. Otherwise, the stockpile might be twice the figure.

If the limited-property-righted houses all over the country and houses uncovered in the statistics also come into the picture, there will be 220 million houses standing in China, including nearly 50 million vacant ones. According to Lin Caiyi, Chief Economist at Guotai Jun'an Securities, the national inventory houses can't sell out in eight years based on the sales rate and marketing diligence over the past year.[1]

The exorbitant inventory in the property market has caused a high concern in the Central Government. At the 11th Meeting of the Central Leading Group for Financial and Economic Affairs on November 10, 2015, General Secretary Xi Jinping stressed that the effort should be made to destock the real estate sector for purpose of sustainable development,[2] and the Executive Meeting of the State Council on November 11 also pointed out that the reform of the household registration system should be accelerated to drive up the consumption in housing and household appliances.

Sharing Economy Approaches to Destock Real Estate Sector

To destock the real estate sector, Tujia.com CEO Luo Jun came out with two approaches: one is to partner the sharing economy platforms and real estate developers through bulk contracts, providing value-added services and enabling developers to sell off those butlered, leased and exchangeable houses; and the other is to activate long-term idle housing on the rental basis via sharing economy platforms which connect developers, owners and consumers.

In 2011, short-term rent platforms like Tujia.com, Airizu.com, Youtx.com and Mayi.com came into being, marking the rise of online

[1] Additional readings: http://gz.house.163.com/15/1123/15/B949TERJ00873C6D.html.

[2] Xi Jinping presided over the 11th Meeting of the Central Leading Group for Financial and Economic Affairs, Xinhuanet: http://news.xinhuanet.com/politics/2015-11/10/c_1117099915.htm.

short-term rent in China; and in 2012, the online short-term rent market in China gained its momentum. According to data from iResearch Consulting, the online short-term rent market came in at RMB 140 million that year. According to the statistics from EnfoDesk, the market expanded close to RMB 3 billion in 2014 and over RMB 10 billion in 2015, with the market growing by more than 50 times in four years. While the hotel market in China was struggling against their development bottlenecks, the online short-term rent market showed a strong growth momentum.

Numerous segments rose rapidly through sharing economy. Statistics show that Xiaozhu.com, a platform mainly specialized in urban short-term rent reservation, had access to over 50,000 houses in more than 200 cities, and it saw its transaction volume at the end of 2015 four times more than that at the beginning of the year. Similarly, the tourism home-stay rent titan Tujia.com also had access to more than 400,000 houses in 2015.

As shown in Fig. 7.1, in the first half of 2015, Tujia.com took the lead in China's online vacation rental market with a share of 41.9%; and it was followed far behind by Xiaozhu.com, Muniao.com, and Youtx.com in order.

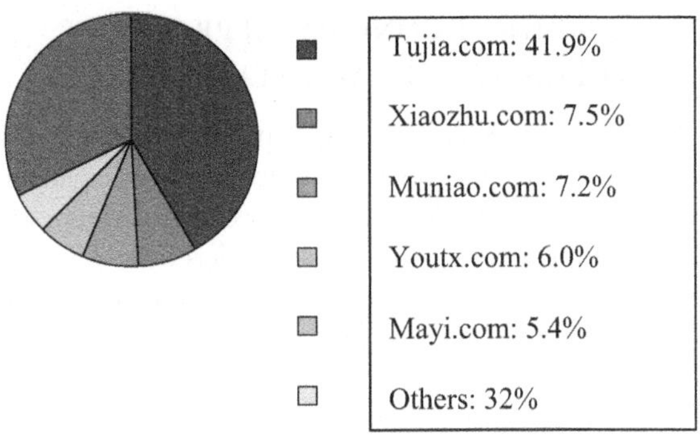

Fig. 7.1 China's online vacation rental market in the first half of 2015 by transaction volume (*Source* EnfoDesk: Short-term Rent Thrives on Both Rising Demands and Supply)

At the Demand Side, a Booming Tourism Fuels the Short-Term Homestay House Rent

According to China National Tourism Administration statistics, tourists made 2.957 billion domestic trips in 2012, generating the revenues of RMB 2.27 trillion for tourism, and 4 billion domestic trips in 2015, generating the revenues of more than RMB 4 trillion for tourism.

Increasingly regarding travel as a way to spice up life and get relief from work stress, travelers increasingly prefer self-guided tours to package tours to get a kick and full fulfillment, and thus each city across the country is no stranger to "backpackers" and "tight-belt tourists". According to the data from the online tourism portal Aoyou.com, the ratio of group tourists against free individual tourists was at about 5.5:4.5 in 2014, up by 5% points compared to the figure of 6:4 in 2013.

However, the outbound tourism boom among Chinese citizens also buoyed up the overseas accommodation short-term rent boat. With 329,000 trips abroad on average each day, Chinese citizens made 120 million outbound trips in 2015, up by 20% year on year. In addition, according to the *Annual Report on Outbound Tourism Development in China*, the accommodation expending for outbound tourists from the Chinese mainland in 2012 largely accounted for 10% of their total outbound tourism budget. Yet, it is inevitable that a pickier demand on accommodation options comes along with the rising demands for travel experience as reflected by the fact that the share of accommodation consumption for Chinese outbound tourists rose to 15% in 2013. Belvedor and Youtx.com, the leading players in the short-term accommodation rent segment in China, provide convenient and comfortable accommodation arrangements to outbound tourists. Airbnb has operated the business in 34,000 cities in more than 190 countries, serving a cumulative total of more than 2 5 million tenants.

The choice of residence is an essential link in travel and a key factor in determining the quality of travel. With the rising fever over self-guided tour, the homestay house short-term rent is gaining popularity among young people. Relative to hotels, the homestay house short-term rent has the following advantages:

- **Price advantage**

Compared to hotels, the short-term rent industry has a unique advantage in price. Houses listed on short-term rent platforms are eligible for residents' price rates in piped water, natural gas, and electricity power supply, which are generally lower than the price rates for hotels. Generally, the rentals for short-term rent houses are also lower than those of hotels, which is one of the important factors for the short-term rent houses to attract consumers.

Short-term rent houses enjoy a marked price advantage, lower than these for comparable hotels by over 40%. A budget hotel room costing RMB 200 is limited to two inhabitants while a short-term rent room with comparable conditions, such as location and quality standard, is limited to four roommates.

- **Personalized experience**

Without the distinct feature of strong rigid demands, short-term rent is simply to satisfy the need for diversified, personalized, and cost-effective accommodation experience. The mode of sharing just serves such a long-tail demand right. In addition, accommodation has a stronger social attribute than travel and also a more obvious non-standardized characteristic.

Despite a bulk of time a day spent at hotel during the travel, the stereotyped settings in virtually all hotels are hard to impress customers. So, Muniao.com turned to competitions based on the "features" of guest rooms. It selected out the rooms or houses with distinctive styles and exquisite layouts so as to deliver lingering impressions on customers and better and nicer experiences for them.

In addition, more travelers are willing to get engaged with strangers from other countries and regions to get a clue of different cultures, customs and so on, make friends of various types, and expand their circles of friends in the context of deepening cultural globalization.

At the Supply Side, an Abundant Supply of Idle Housing Fuels the Short-Term Homestay House Rent

Data show that by the end of 2014, the housing stock in cities and towns in China reached more than 20 billion square meters with more than one unit per household. According to data from Survey and Research Center for China Household Finance, property assets accounted for 69.2% of the total household assets in China in 2015, which is more than twice that in the United States. The long-running housing boom in China has made housing a surplus asset for some residents.

It is also the case in other parts of the world. According to a survey by *The Guardian*, there are more than 11 million vacant houses in Europe, mostly in advanced European economies, such as Spain, France, Italy, and Germany.

Liu Yu, Regional Director at Xiaozhu.com, told reporters, the housing vacancy rate in China is close to 30%, and it is even as high as more than 80% in some resort cities like Sanya. Judging from such figures, the short-term rent market in China is still at the stage of massification and popularization.

The development of the housing rental market is closely related with the ongoing transformation and upgrading in the real estate market. As the stubbornly high housing prices in the past are on a slippery slope now, the good old days of profiting from housing trading will be gone with the wind. The accumulated housing is slow to sell off, more housing holders are forced to turn to other options, thus creating a lot of room for the idle housing rental market to grow from an oversaturated real estate market. In certain regions like Beijing and Shanghai, the gains from short-term rent are even several times as much as those from long-term rent. With a deepening economic downturn, many owners have chosen to rent out their idle houses to gain extra incomes, make their household ends meet, and objectively satisfy the demand from tenants. The practice of such a kind is particularly common in Chinese first-tier cities like Beijing and Shanghai.

Two Major Business Models

C2C Mode (Airbnb and Xiaozhu.com)

Xiaozhu.com, Youtx.com, Mayi.com, and Belvedor are the Chinese answers to Airbnb. The primary feature of their model is that platforms provide a venue for posting information and doing transactions for both housing renters and tenants and they earn a 5–10% commission on completed transactions.

The mode involves three roles, namely, landlords, short-term rent platforms and tenants. Airbnb's rapid development suggests the value of housing sharing. Nowadays, Airbnb provides online rental services in 34,000 cities in 191 countries, gets access to more than 10 million housing units, and is valued at USD 25.5 billion, on par with the top player in the global accommodation sector Hilton Hotel (with a market value of USD 25.52 billion as of August 18, 2015, the same below) and far ahead of Starwood Hotels (with a market value of USD 13.1 billion), InterContinental Hotels &Resorts (with a market value of USD 9.22 billion), and Hyatt Hotels (with a market value of USD 7.57 billion).

C2B2C Mode (Homeway and Tujia.com)

Tujia.com is the Chinese answer to Homeway. It exercises the prescribed control on participating houses, takes charge of their unified decoration and management, and draws its profits from distributed incomes with house owners and other incomes from value-added property services. In such a sense, Tujia.com's business model is more similar to that of traditional hotels. However, given that its cost-saving approach is trusteeship rather than lease, Tujia.com gets its cut of the rental incomes only when tenants check in.

Tujia.com is targeted at the high-end tourism vacation segment, and its participating houses are largely idle houses from individuals and unsold houses from developers on the trusteeship basis, including specialized hotel apartments, villas, and homestay houses.

- **Tenants**

Tujia.com is committed to providing high-quality serviced apartments to meet the diverse accommodation needs from travelers and businessmen in more than 200 cities in China. Unlike short-term rent apartments of all other types, Tujia.com also offers some fringe benefits, such as airport pick-up, kitchenware, as five-star hotels do. In addition, Tujia.com is also aggressive in venturing into overseas markets, and now it even accepts online accommodation booking for its more than 50,000 cost-effective vacation apartments in 96 countries around the world.

All the houses listed on the Tujia.com platform are verified through field inspections and advertised with in-kind real shoots. Besides, Tujia.com also provides a sound "Tenant Safeguard Program" to guarantee that tenants have reliable and secure accommodation experiences.

- **Landlords**

Not only being a free housing promotion platform, Tujia.com is also a diversified service provider for landlords with idle houses. Landlords may post their house information free of charge on the Tujia.com platform or sign in for various services, including house trust and house cleaning and maintenance.

With a large number of houses in hand, its wider market coverage, and its other advantages, Tujia.com quickly emerged as a strong competitor in the short-term rent market. According to statistics, as of the second quarter of 2015, the Tujia.com App had been downloaded by more than 40 million users and hundreds of thousands of inquiries and reservations were made every day via it.

Future Innovations in Short-Term Rent

As a niche segment in the broader accommodation sector, short-term housing rent hasn't reached the stage with higher barriers yet; and it hasn't amassed a widespread market awareness yet. Therefore, it is expected that there will be three trends going forward.

More Diversified Short-Term Rent Landscape[3]

Short-term rent platforms both at home and abroad, such as Airbnb, Tujia.com, Xiaozhu.com, and Belvedor, started with tourism and vacation segments in responding to short-term accommodation needs. However, with those segments increasingly saturated, players are likely to set their eye on the next battleground: business travel.

Besides business travel, there have been new developments at the supply side as short-term house rent is constantly raging in tourism and vacation segments. Demands for transitional short-term house rent from individuals seeking off-site jobs and medical services are increasing in number. Generally, such users are often more price-sensitive and prefer such C2C short-term rent platforms as Xiaozhu.com and Mayi.com.

Focus beyond the social function to non-social ones. For example, in early days, Airbnb focused more on social concepts while landlords preferred to share individual rooms or beds so that all mates engaged in the shared spaces. But later, Airbnb came to realize that accommodation needs widely vary with different sets of users, for example, families, couples, and teams, are more inclined to have the residences alone. As a result, Airbnb adjusted its house type options, adding separate rooms or houses and detached apartments for living alone. Xiaozhu.com CEO Chen Chi estimated that in Airbnb's accommodation sharing occasions, the rate of landlords and tenants living separately has nowadays risen to 75%, a rather high proportion that tends to ever rise.

Mixed Mode Is a Development Trend

- **Blending variations**

The business model of short-term rent comes mainly in two variations: asset-light C2C and asset-heavy C2B2C. Either of the two variations can thrive in the long run, and somewhere in the range of "asset-light" and "asset-heavy" may be the development trend. Tujia.com has already turned from B2C to a mixed variation containing C2C. The aim is to make up for the drawback of its house portfolio highly dominated by

[3] Being Too Challenging to Copy Airbnb: Report on Real Dynamics in Short-term House Rent Market in China, Penguin Intelligence.

standardized house units from developers to further scale up and diversify its house supply and provide a social interaction platform between landlords and users.

- **Extending the industrial chain**

To extend the industrial chain through strategic partnership. The alliance between Tujia.com and its likes with aligned purposes helps reintegrate business models from hotel operation to short-term house rental and long-term house rental to incorporate more diverse operations from real estate to finance, crowd-funding and other projects in the future.

- **Issues about middleman landlords**

As Airbnb expands its global presence, its users increases rapidly thus its house sources also need to be expanded rapidly. However, some homeowners have not access to the Internet for various reasons, so "middleman landlords" with houses on their hands are becoming the cooperators.

The middleman landlords in the USA, also known as Property Manager or Realty Manager, are different from "middleman landlords" in China, and sometimes they work with OTAs in housing distribution.

Yet, the cooperation between middleman landlords and Airbnb is under regulatory pressure. The *Los Angeles Times* reported that under pressure from communities and social groups, the US housing authorities had stepped up their scrutiny of Airbnb, which was forced to curtail its cooperation with professional landlords. For example, two biggest homeowners in the Los Angeles, which have dozens of holiday-rental apartments, and other homeowners were delisted in April from the platform of Airbnb.

In addition, there are legal restrictions on middleman landlords. A San Francisco law makes it clear that before re-renting a house, a re-renter is required to inform the owner and obtain his consent. No re-rental should be made if such a transaction isn't permitted in the original rental agreement. The re-rental price shall not exceed the original rental price and the offender shall be fined USD 1,000 per day. French laws provide that owners can legally rent their main residence when they are away on holiday. However, the owner will have to pay a travel tax on the rented house if he has a second residence.

CHAPTER 8

Ownership Surplus

In many people's minds, sharing economy is to share access; that is, to lease. Since a second-handed item transaction is about the transfer of its ownership, how can it be sharing economy?

Actually, from the perspective of economics, excess ownership can also be shared. Based on ownership surplus, secondhand item transactions improve the utilization of items and prolong their service life. Additionally, there are roughly two forms of secondhand item trading: trading with intermediaries and trading without intermediaries. The former is the traditional model, and the latter is our focus: it is also known as point-to-point second-handed item trading, where buyers and sellers make transactions directly on a trading platform. Driven by the profit-making nature, intermediaries tend to do anything they can to widen the price differences; and thus, the former usually end up in a loss to both buyers and sellers while the latter form is the product from the internet, and thus contributes to lower transaction costs, ending up with a gain for both parties involved in a transaction.

"Lemon Market" of Traditional Trading

What about the market for used car transactions with intermediaries? It's a typical "lemon market". Due to the information asymmetry caused by intermediaries who knows more information than the buyers and the

M. Huateng et al., *The Chinese Sharing Economy*,
https://doi.org/10.1007/978-981-33-6494-3_8

sellers, the market is inefficient—shigh-quality goods are classified as inferior here and valued at lower levels, forming a vicious cycle that "bad money drives out good". The traditional used car market is fraught with such problems as information asymmetry and complex trading chains. On the one hand, sellers have a lower bargaining power than intermediaries; on the other hand, buyers dare not "dip a toe into the muddy waters" in the mixed situation, hence the assumption that all used cars are inferior. Therefore, sellers either choose not to sell such used cars or sell them to the dealers at lower prices, or at a loss of about 30% to intermediaries.

Sharing economy carves out a reasonable alternative to the lemon market. Cutting off intermediaries such as 4S stores, dealers and distributors from the trading process, it provides a platform for direct transactions between buyers and sellers, eliminates information barriers, forges a transparent and standardized trading process and solves the lemon market dilemma, thus slashing the trading costs by at least 5–7% for buyers and driving up the closing prices by more than 10% for sellers.

Used car e-commerce platforms came into being in 2010, and Cheyipai.com, the first used car online trading platform in China, was launched that year. Since 2013, the market has gained pace, and attracted keen interest from venture capital, with iconic forerunners, like Cheyipai.com and Uxin.com, receiving multiple rounds of investments. Not to be outdone, some conglomerates set up their own online trading platforms for used cars, including Ping'an Group's Pahaoche.com, SAIC Group's CXusedcar.com, etc.

By 2015, the e-commerce market for used cars entered into the stage of explosive growth. According to the statistics from the China Passenger Car Association (CPCA), 8.403 million sets of used cars worth RMB 492.421 billion changed hands from January 2015 to November of the same year, registering a YoY growth margin of 3.63%. Especially in November of that year alone, 846,400 sets of used cars worth RMB 50.299 billion changed hands, with the transaction volume and amount up by 17.52 and 24.76% month on month respectively.

China's used car trading market is still much smaller than its peers in developed countries. According to statistics, in contrast to being 2–3 times the trading volume of new cars in developed markets, the used car trading volume in China is only 1/3 of the new car trading volume. However, such a gap also indicates that China's used car trading market is likely to continue to develop.

Along with development and maturation over years, business models have also increased and varied in the online used car market, including the C2C mode integrating "on-site inspection + online trading + car delivery" at Renrenche.com, the mode integrating "B2B online/offline auction + B2C online retail" at Uxin.com, and the B2B mode integrating "offline car inspection + online platform auction + offline car delivery & service" at www.Cheyipai.com, just name a few.

By enabling direct engagement between buyers and sellers, Renrenche.com acts as a third-party platform for transactions. Without troubling the sellers, it fulfills photo-taking, pricing, inspecting (into 249 items), testing and assessing of used cars at sellers' premises and issues written inspection and appraisal reports. Car information, pictures, and prices are posted on the official website for the buyers to check. Besides, it is also responsible for picking up buyers to examine cars and verify their conditions, prices, and other items in inspection reports on the spot so as to facilitate transactions. It conducts very detailed bench-testing on traded cars in the face of both parties, and fulfills the necessary transfer procedures for the trading parties if no disagreement, or organizes renegotiation between the three parties on disagreed issues.

As an intermediary, Renrenche.com is responsible for main tasks: collecting car information at sellers' premises, assisting sellers in determining prices, taking buyers to check cars on the spot, providing car information to buyers, assisting buyers with car inspections; going through transfer and registration procedures for trading parties.

Renrenche.com reaps a 3% cut of the transaction price as a commission (subject to the RMB 2000–8000 range), far below the 10–15% cut at brick-and-mortar car dealers. In addition, buyers are entitled to the platform's commitments, including the free maintenance policy (within 20,000 km mileage or one year of the purchase) and no-hassle return policy (within 14 days of the purchase). Sellers make the least input of time and effort and are released of all responsibilities once their cars change hands, while buyers are also assisted in checking car conditions and determining prices, and can rest assured with sufficient after-sale warranty.

In its C round of financing led by Tencent Strategy in August 2015, Renrenche.com raised USD 85 million and escalated its post-money valuation to more than USD 500 million. Besides, it is also the second BAT-backed (Baidu, Alibaba, Tencent) e-commerce platform for used cars in China.

Driving Forces of a Flourishing Secondary Trading Market

In the era of commodity economy, consumers, especially young people, are prone to impulsive consumption amid numerous shopping sprees meticulously orchestrated by merchants. Lured by lower prices, the hilarious atmosphere during holidays, and other factors, they tend to buy blindly things that are seldom used only to accumulate a lot of idle products. Second-handed item trading carves out an outlet for impulsive consumers, enabling them to resell their idle items to others with a higher demand and recover a certain proportion of costs. Besides, with the rapid upgrading of goods, many items soon become idle ones. Secondhand item trading gives these idle items the chance to bring out their surplus value to full play to meet the needs of different populations. A lot of things for emergencies also are no longer needed, becoming idle items to be disposed of. Secondary trading just does the work to increase their mobility and improve their utilization rate. Secondary trading is in line with the concept of "environmental conservation and recycling".

Changed social customs make the use of secondhand items no longer an embarrassment and even a "fashion". High commodity prices, especially rising costs of living in big cities, drive down the demands for goods with a high demand elasticity, such as high-end goods. Therefore, second-handed items simply offer a trade-off between high tastes and low prices in meeting the needs of many consumers.

Two Models of Secondary Trading

From sharing economy perspective, the operating models of secondhand item trading platforms are roughly classified into two main groups: barter and paid acquisition.

Yerdle is a typical barter platform for trading secondhand items, where users can get items for free on the platform except for logistics fees. Any secondhand item transactions on the platform do not involve payments in cash, and users only win "credit points" from selling their goods. New users are granted credit points from the platform, and amass their additional credit points through the purchase and sale of items on the platform. The credit point approach is, in fact, another form of the credit system. While operating its sharing economy platform, Yerdle is also creating a new credit system and shaping a complete business model.

Websites with similar business models include Swaptree and Freecycle, but we have no such platforms in China.

Another group is more popular: paid acquisition, that is, buyers pay for idle items from sellers via the internet to complete a secondary transaction. Taobao Xianyu, Liangyi Hui, Paipai.com, and Zhuanzhuan.com fall into such a category. Take Taobao Xianyu platform as an example. As long as you are a Taobao user, you can log in directly to the website, directly resell your "babies" (a nickname for your idle items). Sellers set up a "site of transfer" on the platform for posting their related information, such as their locations and contact information. At the same time, the platform also publishes information related to the transactions, including a user's purchase records and the credit points to provide safeguards to the creditworthiness and transaction security. Represent platforms of such a kind abroad include Poshmark, a clothing trading platform, and Kidizen, a trading platform for children's goods.

Prospect of Secondary Trading

According to estimates from SMZDM.com, an online shopping recommendation website, second-handed item transactions accounted for about 0.8% of the total retail sales in 2013 in the USA. If the penetration rate of second-handed item trading in China reached such a level in 2015, based on RMB 18.3 trillion of retail sales in the same year, it was reckoned that China's second-handed item market in 2015 stood at about RMB 146.2 billion. If we factored in the long-running clogged channels of circulation, the market for second-handed items might be much greater than the estimated.

At present, the secondary trading platform sector in China shows a sound development trend, and its capital market maintains a high degree of activity. Xianyu, which already has more than 50,000 trading communities, is estimated to have raised more than USD 3 billion in capital markets in 2015 and saw more than 200,000 idle items change hands every day. Moreover, Liangyi Huihui also received RMB 3 million in its angel round financing, Panghu, a trading platform for used luxury goods, also garnered RMB 10 million from angel investors at the end of 2015.

The special attribute of secondhand items also brings the hidden worries over online transactions, especially a series of problems relating to commodity quality. While the P2P model facilitates information communication between buyers and sellers, given the quality and other conditions of secondhand items are difficult to assess, a wide variety of goods on comprehensive trading platforms, it is actually difficult in getting full knowledge of secondhand items relying on online information alone. Generally, consumers have to assess the authenticity, quality, and sources of secondhand items on their own. What's more, both sellers and platforms can't provide after-sales services on secondhand items. So, there are still risks with buying second-handed items.

One of the priorities for the secondary trading industry in the future is to build its own platform brand and accumulate a stable user base. Moreover, with the sources of products holding the key, secondary trading platforms should implement more standardized processes and methods, keep strict control over the sources, quality, types and other conditions of second-handed items, and effectively protect the rights and interests of consumers.

CHAPTER 9

Sharing Time Surplus: Playing Multiple Roles is in Vogue

In 2016, you can no longer need a "Nine-to-Five" job. Perhaps, you can be a free man wearing many hats or start a business and become "your own boss". As playing multiple roles are in vogue, you may make such a decision.

In the era of planned economy, jobs and professional roles are generally considered to be the same things, and your job is virtually the same as your career life. While in the era of market economy, jobs no longer function like a screw that always stays put. Roles and jobs started to split but roles, more often than not, remain supplements to jobs. Yet, jobs have lost ground to professional roles in the era of sharing economy.

Since you can translate your work, knowledge, skill, technology, management expertise, and experience into real benefits anytime and anywhere through the Internet, why should you bind yourself to a nine-to-five job agreement? In the traditional employment theory, no employment agreement means unemployment. But nowadays, it may be a different picture. An "unemployed" you may, all the same, have multiple "roles" to play: not only earning your incomes and realizing your values but also creating wealth for the society. With a booming sharing economy, permanent jobs are disappearing, and playing temporary professional roles is becoming a commonplace. Sharing personal idle resources has delivered a major impact on the traditional employment model.

With the popularity of sharing economy, the supply of and demands for a large number of temporary jobs may be matched on the Internet

M. Huateng et al., *The Chinese Sharing Economy*,
https://doi.org/10.1007/978-981-33-6494-3_9

platforms, such as Crowdsourcing and Witkey. Various professional roles, including private chefs, private foreign tutors, private doctors, private assistants, private consultants and private logisticians, are becoming very popular on the internet, luring more and more people to try their lucks in such a new field.

Private Chefs

Private Chefs refer to the chefs or workers who cook for individual customers, or the customized cuisines. Relying on Internet platforms, the private chef culture is gradually stepping into the public view, and is in immense vogue in first- and second-tier cities in China. On platforms, private chefs share their cuisines with others, gain a sense of fulfillment while earning incomes, and diners make friends while enjoying all kinds of delicious foods. This practice not just contributes to the full use of labor resources, but also to changes in lifestyles.

According to the Prospective Industry Research Institute's *Analysis Report on 2015–2020 Internet Catering Industry Business Models and Investment Strategy Planning in China*, over the past two years, China's private chef sharing market has been accumulating strength and scaling up, girding up its loins for explosive development. The driving forces behind the massive development of the private chef sector over recent years are listed as follows:

First, saving time

As we all know, people in big cities have to work more than eight hours every day, and so have no much extra time for grocery shopping and cooking. The fast pace of work and life for middle-/high-income populations in first-tier cities leads to the rising demand for having chefs doing the cooking at home, thus providing a prime chance for private chef sharing platforms to enter the vision of the public.

Second, having a higher cost-efficiency

According to promotional handouts from some at-home private chefs, the service prices are as follows: RMB 69–79 for a set meal of four dishes plus a soup, RMB 99–109 for a set meal of six dishes plus a bowl of soup, and RMB 129–169 for a set meal of eight dishes plus a bowl of soup. Therefore, reasonable price levels make the new market a desirable option for ordinary households. Also, the realization of "having a ready-cooked meal" desire is an important reason for more and more consumers to have a try.

Third, delivering a nicer and more participatory dining experience
With the constant improvement in life over recent years, the private chef pattern focuses more on the dining atmosphere and considerate services, thus providing a new dining option and delivering a nicer and more participatory dining experience to consumers.

Fourth, having higher convenience
Authentic featured cuisines specific to various localities are virtually found in the kitchens of ordinary residents. While migrating into a city, foreigners from all over the world also bring with them the authentic cooking back in their hometowns, and so can satisfy the taste buds of their new fellow urban residents. Without any trouble of venturing out of their own cities, urban residents can have a taste of the most authentic cuisines and their Anecdotal tales in other regions, such as Sichuan-style cuisines, Yunnan-style cuisines, Canton-style cuisines and so on.

Fifth, building up a social sphere
Since ancient times, a "dinner party" has been the centerpiece of social scenes in China. In modern times, social circles are getting smaller and smaller due to higher work pressure. To know a group of like-minded strangers by enjoying a meal together can make friends, expanding one's life circle and developing one's networks of relationships. Some survey data shows that both private chefs and their users have a strong desire for social contacts. One of their biggest expectations from a private chef-arranged dinner is to be able to meet new friends and increase their contacts. Private Chefs are also willing to deliver more added values to their customers by organizing themed social events.

The private chef market mainly consists of four service models: in-store service for social meals, at-home cooking service, e-commerce service for consignment sales and O2O takeout service. The market is still in its infancy and has no obviously dominant players. Among various service models, the homely dish takeout service, which caters to recurring rigid demands, seems to have a more promising development prospect.

According to EnfoDesk statistics, the internet catering take-out market in China reached RMB 45.78 billion in 2015, and Baidu Takeaway, Ele.me, and Meituan.com were in the dominant position, with their combined market share up to 85.8%. With the market so huge, the remaining 14.2% of the market still amounts to RMB 6.5 billion, so there is still an immense piece of market space left for the homely dish takeout service to grab. Players rushed into the homely dish take-out market in various directions: Mishi focused on dish take-out service following the C2C food e-commerce model, Shaofanfan tried to satisfy "taste buds" by diversifying beyond the at-home service to take-out service, Edaixi.com redeveloped Xiaoeguanjia.com into Xiaoeguanfan.com, and Douguo.com launched its online e-commerce platform Ushihui.cn for selling semi-finished food materials to significantly drive up its sales of semi-finished stuff.

Amid the fierce competition in private chef service fief full of numerous players, how to open up and dominate new segments, scale up faster, grab outsize say and diversify service variations to meet the needs of consumers in multiple scenarios is the future direction of development.

Private Tutor

Internet effectively connects education providers and learners, disrupting the asymmetric information predicament in the education sector. A private tutor is a rising role of sharing economy in this sector. For example, a teacher living in New York can teach a kid in Beijing an oral English lesson, introducing disruptive changes in online English training.

As online teaching goes viral, VIPABC website has developed new offerings of this kind in over 80 cities in more than 60 countries through over 500 native teachers in the U.K. and USA, providing live online services around the clock to learners. So far, VIPABC has offered more than 10 million sessions of online English learning to English learners, making remarkable results.

Dr. Yang Zhenda, CEO of VIPABC, said that we will open up our platform to global users, and in future, no matter what skills you have, yoga, cooking, or any others, and no matter anytime and anywhere, you can share them through our platform. The era of the on-demand selection of either experts or consumers has been around here.

In addition to professionals in other sectors who can offer part-time lectures during their free time, regular teachers in schools can also offer online teaching services. For example, Afanti100.com invites public school teachers as part-time instructors at Q&A sessions, helping narrow differences in teacher resources among various regions, Changingedu.com provides the services of tutor search and one-on-one at-home tutoring, and Genshuixue.com forges a whole closed loop of knowledge acquisition, question answering and offline services by integrating online and offline approaches.

Sharing economy in the education sector has changed the distribution imbalance of educational resources in time and space. Traditional sharing economy models have expanded the incremental market of educational resources and improved the efficiency of matching the supply and demands while emerging sharing economy models are innovating educational models. Sharing economy in the education sector is just beginning to bloom.

Private Doctors

In China, strained doctor-patient relationships are the focus of social attention. Along with the combination of sharing economy and medical service industry, doctors can not only share basic medical services during their spare time but also can embrace various emerging models, such as offering their services at various clinics or offering their services by paying visits to their patients. At the same time, hospitals and clinics can also leverage their idle resources to broaden the access to affordable medical services, forge a seamless offline closed-loop of mobile medical treatment, and promote the hierarchical medical treatment system.

Under the traditional medical system, the medical devices and materials of a hospital are its own property, and many precision instruments and equipment often stay idle. Take hospital beds as an example. According to the National Health and Family Planning Commission statistics, the utilization rate of hospital beds across the country was 88.0% in 2014. To be specific, 92.8% at public hospitals, 63.1% at private hospitals, 60.1% at first-level hospitals, 60.5% at rural hospitals, 55.6% at community medical centers, and 101.8% at Class-III grade-A hospitals.

The role of private doctor comes in two typical models:

First, Chunyu.me Model

With the development of online consultation platforms, such as Chunyu.me, DXY.com, Ping'an Health, and Haodf.com, part-time doctors on crowdsourcing platforms can provide real-time and convenient remote consultation services, answering questions online for simple diseases and providing referral channels for complex diseases. In the future, outpatient demand for physical medical resources will be greatly reduced, and other on-site routines, including registration and waiting for seeing doctors, will be replaced by online procedures, thus greatly reducing the time for medical services.

Doctors can share their medical knowledge and build personal brands in their spare time, and hospitals can employ their accumulated user resources to produce greater marketing values. For patients, doctors can answer patients' questions online and give advice. Questions from patients are very convergent, so structured data may be used for advice on diagnosis and treatment.

Second, At-home Service Model

Private doctors providing at-home medical services have been around abroad, like Medicast. Medicast can provide users with customized medical solutions, set up technology platforms for hospitals, connect doctors and patients quickly through online platforms, and have patients get timely access to at-home services fit with their unique conditions.

There are similar trends in China. Three entities: Alibaba Group's Ali Health, Didi Chuxing, and Mingyizhudao.com, partnered in pioneering at-home services for two days in Beijing, Shanghai, Hangzhou, and Nanjing in 2015, and offered "Didi Doctor" at-home services to more than 2000 users in these cities.

Sharing economy has broad prospects in the medical service sector. The *Policy Measures to Promote the Accelerated Development of Privately-run Medical Services* issued in June 2015 by the General Office of the State Council clearly stated that efforts should be made to promote the circulation and sharing of medical resources, promote the joint financing and sharing of large medical equipment, promote the multi-site practice of doctors, strengthen business cooperation, and accelerate the common development of public and private medical institutions through mutual support. Deepening the reform of the medical service system will open up more room for development to private doctors.

Private Assistant

Traditional Witkey services are mainly oriented to enterprises. As the Witkey model goes viral, the traditional one of "*All Are Full-time Employees and All Are Done on the Premises*" has become outdated. Nowadays, enterprises can break through various constraints, including geographical, industry, or professional factors, to tap desired professionals flexibly and transition to the business models of virtual enterprises. For example, ZBJ.com, a professional service enterprise in China, has grown into a unicorn. Not limited to the Witkey communities, any willing individuals with related skills can become virtual employees of an enterprise through this crowd-sourcing service.

Now, the model has taken new twists. Sharing economy provides more and more individual service providers with job openings and all types of C2C private service platforms targeting market segments, therefore, on one hand effectively liberating labors with skills, interests and idle time, and on the other, fully satisfying unique needs from users in personalization and convenience.

The typical platforms, Nishuowoban in China and TaskRabbit, are both crowd-sourcing platforms focusing on local comprehensive life services. TaskRabbit made its marks by running errands and doing chores, such as queuing and dog-walking for others. Users post their demands and ceiling prices on the platform, bidders made responses, and the platform finally determines the most suitable candidates based on various factors, including comprehensive prices, distances, and skills.

Besides the private assistant service model focusing on running errands, the private old-age caretaker service model is also taking shape.

Private Caretaker

Being home to the largest old-age population (with more than 100 million senior citizens), China is also one of the fastest aging countries in the world. According to the international aging society criterion of over 60 years old population accounting for 10% of the total population, or over 65 years old population accounting for 7% of the total population, China has been an aging society since 2000. According to China National Committee on Ageing's projections, aging in China will speed up at the average annual increase rate of 10 million persons over the next 20 years until 2050, when its old age population is expected to account for one-third of its total population.

With the greatest aging market potential in the world, China has much to be improved in its senior citizen care-taking sector.

According to a 36Kr report, Paibama (an old-age care-taking entity in China) waded into the home-based old-age care-taking sector by the sharing economy approach: they organized hundreds of medical staff into the communities to provide medical consultation services, namely, "home-based medical inspections conducted by community doctors + hospital visits accompanied by staff at community hospitals", to meet the rigid demand for the elderly health management.

In addition to community doctors, the platform also brings together a group of new graduates in elderly caretaking and nursing to play the role of "Health Manager". Each community is usually taken care of by 20–30 health managers. At a service appointment, a health manager will come over to determine the needs of the elderly and decide whether or not services are needed from medical staff. Moreover, they also provide various real-time services, such as on-site consultations, rehabilitation care, health education, Chinese medicine acupuncture, physical testing, chronic disease management, etc. The services not only can eliminate the need of visiting hospitals, queuing up and waiting for medical services, but also help the elderly prevent diseases and treat minor illnesses at home.

Private Consultant

Zhaihang is an interesting website. Have you ever talked to strangers about your troubles or traveled with strangers in strange cities? Zhaihang is such a social networking site that allows you to have a nice and candid moment with strangers.

Netizens commented: "helping common person out through socialized crowd-sourcing is the greatest value of sharing economy". According to a Huxiu.me report, the purpose of Zhaihang is to solve the needs of personalized knowledge that existing searches, communities, and other network channels fail to meet and share personalized experiences. It focuses on one-to-one face-to-face communication and enables the exchange of a large amount of information in a short period of time. The founding expert team at Zhaihang is ready to share and good at communication, and it has the traits of "sharing personality", that is, they take the delight in helping others with their wisdom and expertise. The case of them is another confirmation on the "cognitive surplus" theory. We have many similar platforms out there, for example, Skillshare, Zide, and Bangyang, to name just a few.

Private Logistician

At the Fifth Annual Conference of Chinese Electronic Commerce and Logistics Entrepreneurs, Xie Qin, CEO of Rrkd.cn, said that Rrkd.cn is a product under the "Internet Plus" sharing economy system, and its core purpose is to do the picking-up for others in spare time to meet the need of low-cost distribution. In the future, Rrkd.cn will strive to have everyone take part in express delivery and sales, making it a mass fad, namely, everyone can be a salesman to meet the needs of their friends and himself, truly realizing the dream of being one's own boss.

The idea of "mass express delivery" exactly embodies the meaning of the role of a private logistician. As a result, therefore, Rrkd.cn focuses on providing to individuals with services like "taking delivery at a specified time" and "buying on my behalf" by combining socialized logistics and socialized sales. Dada, another logistics platform, is also pioneering an innovative practice: location-based logistics services to small-/medium-sized vendors, where deliverymen take in orders, pick up goods, and deliver goods based on LB information.

The private logistician service not only makes a hit but also achieves some breakthroughs in the inter-city express delivery sector.

Space Bus is a technological service platform in the era of express delivery 2.0, which rallies idle social resources to complete a task of express delivery within the same day, also known as the crowdsourcing logistics model. In fact, it is another form of expression of sharing economy in the express delivery sector. Space Bus is to rally idle "personal" resources for solving the issue of time efficiency in long-distance cross-city express delivery by taking advantage of passengers' idle carriage capacity for small items while traveling by high-speed rail train or air flight. For individual passengers, it not only spices up their journeys but also brings them extra incomes. It usually takes 2–3 days for ordinary express firms to deliver an item to a destination in another city, and even the fastest SF Express service has the difficulty in completing cross-city transportation of an item within the same day. Still, Space Bus can accomplish such a feat even within 9 hours. Being eager to land their hands on their mailed items, users are ready to pay price premiums to meet their requirements on time efficiency.[1]

Known as "last-mile distribution", intra-city freight transport has huge room for development to be tapped. Differing from the nationally networked logistics services, intra-city freight transport is to provide short-haul logistics services within a city, drastically reducing logistics

[1] Additional Readings: http://b2b.toocle.com/detail--6292978.html.

costs, improving logistics efficiency, and effectively slashing the no-load operation of numerous trucks on their return way in urban logistics.

Non-standardized services more effectively meet personalized needs. With a quicker life pace, mounting work pressure, fragmented time slots, and rising aspiration for life quality, the service model of "buying on behalf of others and delivery" is becoming more popular. In the context of sharing economy, connecting the two polarized classes: busy rich men and idle poor men via sharing platforms will not only leverage fragmented time slots but also to a certain extent reduce the waste of social resources.

PART III

Impact: Supply-Side Reform

The sharing economy is intimately linked to the structural reforms that China is currently pursuing. The sharing economy can boost the utilization of existing resources, increase aggregate supply, consumer purchasing power, and consumption demand, thus providing new approaches for macroeconomic restructuring.

In 2015, the central government proposed supply-side reforms that would transform the forces of growth in the Chinese economy, and turn the service sector into the main source of economic growth. The sharing economy provides a new perspective from which to approach supply-side reform. Two windows of opportunity have emerged: the clearing of real estate inventory and the upgrading of the service sector.

From the perspective of the first window of opportunity, the sharing economy offers a new solution for clearing real estate inventory, in the form of the"rent-to-own" model. There are 220 million new completed houses in China, with nearly 50 million vacant houses. Total real estate inventory has reached 686 million m^2. At the current rate of sales, it will take at least 8 years to clear all existing inventory. What solution does the sharing economy prescribe? Tujia has adopted two approaches. First, sharing economy platforms collaborate with developers, inking agreements to sell inventory housing in batches. This provides value-added services to developers, and promotes the sale of properties that offer butler services, leasing, and that are exchangeable. Second, sharing economy platforms have developed the rent-to-own model. By connecting developers, owners and consumers, the platforms are able to satisfy various forms of rental demand, thereby reviving inventory housing that have long been idle in a somewhat roundabout way.

From the perspective of the second window of opportunity, the sharing economy provides new growth drivers for the service sector, thus substantially promoting structural adjustment. This is manifested in three regards: First, the sharing economy transforms idle inventory into new supply capacity through online social platforms. For example, resources owned by an individual, such as residential property, personal vehicles, capital, knowledge, experience and skills, can play a role in matching overall supply and demand while reducing transaction costs. Second, consumption demand is effectively boosted. Take the case of passenger transport. In Beijing, a city of more than 20 million people, there are only 60,000 taxis. Platforms such as Didi and Uber expand overall transport capacity by allowing millions of private cars to enter the market, allowing consumption to increase by a factor of dozens. Third, the sharing economy has generated a great many jobs. Emerging online employment and crowdsourcing express delivery platforms, chiefly represented by zbj.com and rrkd.cn, have created upwards of 30 million jobs. All in all, the various sharing economy platforms have provided new growth drivers for the service sector by creating new facilitating conditions.

Moreover, the sharing economy has altered traditional modes of employment, created new forms of work and opportunities, and relieved downward pressures on employment caused by supply-side reforms.

The sharing economy can also increase resource utilization, reduce resource consumption, and ease the rate of resource exploitation. The environmental sector also benefits when the new energy industry is incorporated into the sharing economy. Despite the somewhat complex relationship between pollution and the sharing economy, we shall adopt a dialectical perspective towards this problem in the following chapter.

From an ontological perspective, the emergence of the term "sharing economy" requires that we revisit the definition of an "economy". The British have demonstrated foresight in this regard. In *The Sharing Economy in the UK*, it was noted that the economic benefits generated by the sharing economy are not included in official GDP accounting. Yet, despite the rapid growth of the sharing economy, it is impossible to track its contribution towards economic growth simply through official data. This is true not only for the UK, but also throughout the entire world, including China.

CHAPTER 10

Increasing Supply

There are two ways to increase supply capacity: (1) increase the utilization of idle resources; (2) generate new sources of supply.

Increasing Resource Utilization

Let us first start from the beloved private car.

Before the advent of ride-hailing apps, private cars spent most of their time idle. According to figures from road transport authorities, the average mileage of a private car in China is roughly 200,000 km, whereas the average mileage of a taxi is greater than 600,000 km, because private cars spend far less time on the road than taxis.

Let's say you own a car and decide to become a Didi driver. What would be the change to your car's utilization rate?

Before joining Didi, a driver may drive for 1 hour per day. After becoming a Didi driver, he may drive an additional 0.13 hours each day. Obviously, his vehicle's utilization rate has increased by 13%.

The assumption that a driver is on the road for 1 hour per day originates from an article in the *Study Times* published on December 1, 2015, according to which a light passenger vehicle in China remains idle for 23 hours per day.

That a driver would be on the road for 1.13 hours per day after joining Didi is an estimate. The *Big Data Report on Smart Travel in China 2015* reveals that 1.43 billion rides were hailed through the Didi platform in

M. Huateng et al., *The Chinese Sharing Economy*,
https://doi.org/10.1007/978-981-33-6494-3_10

2015, translating to 490 million driving hours. It is estimated that more than 10 million vehicles are registered on the Didi platform. Thus, 4.9 ÷ 0.1 ÷ 365 = 0.13, meaning that the average Didi-registered vehicle spends 0.13 additional hours on the road. According to the *China Mobile Ride-Hailing Applications Market Research Report 2014–2015* released by CNIT-Research, roughly 450 million people in China (out of a total population of 1.3 billion) have daily commuting needs, including the 30 to 50 million people who take taxis or hail private cars through ride-sharing platforms. This implies a person-to-vehicle ratio of 40:1 (1.3 billion/30 million).

Take Beijing for instance, a mega-city with a permanent population of over 20 million. Based on a person-to-vehicle ratio of 40:1, at least 500,000 taxis are required, while there are only 66,000 taxis in Beijing, a number that has remained unchanged since 2003. This is far from enough to meet daily commuting needs.

In addition to private cars, idle passenger and goods vehicles are also deployed in fields such as urban logistics (flow of goods within the same city). Urban logistics platforms, including G7 Freighter, Logistics QQ Truck Help, Yunniao Distribution, Huolala, 1HHD.com, and Lanxiniu, have increased the utilization rate of motor vehicles, supplementing the limited capacity of freight vehicles, and greatly enhancing resource utilization.

This principle also applies to other fields.

Generating New Sources of Supply

In the past, society's total supply capacity was mainly provided by enterprises. Today, individuals now contribute towards overall supply capacity. Private cars are merely the tip of the iceberg.

When idle resources are shared by individuals and enterprises, there will be an increase in aggregate supply, even if factories are not producing new cars, clothes or other commodities, and developers are not building new buildings.

Take tourist accommodation for instance. Previously, tourists could only stay in hotels or guesthouses, which were often fully booked during peak seasons. Now, online platforms allow tourists to rent private residences on a short-term basis, which has given an instant boost to the total supply of tourist accommodation. In a way, this supply is practically unlimited. According to its CEO, Luo Jun, since the official launch of

Tujia.com on December 1, 2011, the portal now covers 288 destinations in mainland China and 353 foreign destinations (including the regions of Hong Kong and Taiwan). More than 400,000 residential properties are registered on Tujia.com, including apartments, villas, and homestays. At present, the company has signed agreements with 172 Chinese government agencies and launched strategic collaborations with many Chinese real estate developers. The company now has a reserve of more than 600,000 residential properties under "contracted management", with a total value exceeding 1 billion yuan. Negotiations on more than 10,000 residential projects are ongoing. It is expected that 1 million properties will be registered on Tujia.com in the near future. One cannot help but be excited at these figures. Isn't this the rise of a new supply capacity?

Apart from Tujia.com, there are several startups involved in the market for short-term rentals of residential properties, including mayi.com and muniao.com, which have each developed nearly 300,000 "boutique properties" that span more than 300 Chinese cities.

According to official data from Tujia.com, 6% of the landlords of 50 million vacant residential properties (the figure of 50 million was obtained from figures released by the Economic Research Institute of the State Council) are willing to lease their properties on a short-term basis through online platforms. This means that there will be at least 3 million additional properties entering the online short-term rental market in the near future, which will greatly increase the supply of tourist accommodation in China.

CHAPTER 11

Boosting Demand

From the perspective of demand, the sharing economy can enhance the real purchasing power and welfare of consumers, thereby spurring growth in consumption, creating new sources of growth in the face of downward economic pressures.

Raising Real Purchasing Power

In general, two factors contribute towards an increase in real purchasing power: (1) lower costs; (2) greater incomes. The sharing economy can boost consumers' real purchasing power in two aspects.

Lower Costs

Cost reductions can be made in two aspects. First, reduction of direct costs. The sharing economy is an Internet-based platform economy. Platforms eliminate information asymmetry and match supply and demand, while also getting rid of complex procedures and expensive intermediary fees, thereby reducing transaction costs and enhancing the real purchasing power of consumers. Second, reduction of the costs of selection. For example, the cost of homestay is obviously much cheaper than a five-star hotel. According to the current pricing of budget hotels in China, a standard room costs 150 to 300 yuan per day, a normal suite costs 400 to 700 yuan per day, and a presidential suite costs 1500 to 3000 yuan

M. Huateng et al., *The Chinese Sharing Economy*,
https://doi.org/10.1007/978-981-33-6494-3_11

per day. In comparison, we can rent a room for less than 100 yuan per day on short-term rental platforms. Renting an entire apartment, which has several rooms, costs only 100 to 800 yuan. Daily rent for a bungalow, (200 m^2 or more) costs merely 800 to 3000 yuan.

A research team led by Prof. Georgios Zervas of Boston University found that, in the face of competition from Airbnb, traditional hotels usually adopt price reduction strategies, which is especially the case among medium- and low-end hotels. Airbnb users are sensitive to prices. For traditional hotels, price discounts are a good way to retain consumers. In this way, all travelers (including Airbnb users) benefit from Airbnb's price discount strategies, because they now enjoy a lower cost of accommodation.

Some may harbor doubts about some sectors of the sharing economy. For instance, private kitchens offer meals that cost more per diner than in ordinary restaurants. How do we ascertain that the sharing economy does indeed reduce intermediary fees and costs?

This is a dialectical issue which requires that we consider different reference systems. However, there is no denying that several platforms which operate on a shared kitchen model, such as Mishi, Woyoufan, and Go Home to Eat, are able to avoid expenses such as rental for a conventional restaurant space and wages for service staff. The price advantages of the private kitchen model may be as obvious when compared to comparable fare in the same price range and dining environment, but they offer greater quality assurances compared to ordinary restaurants, not to mention the benefits of social interaction that they offer, which cannot be measured in monetary terms.

Greater Income

The sharing economy provides the general public with a way to engage in economic activities through nearby resources, thereby generating new channels for wealth circulation. As members of the sharing economy, consumers can obtain extra income outside of regular employment, thus increasing their overall income. This increases their real purchasing power in absolute terms to a certain extent (inflation aside).

Forbes magazine estimated that direct flow of income to participants in the sharing economy totaled USD 3.5 billion in 2013, a year-on-year increase of 25%.

According to a study of Airbnb by Gene Sperling, a former Assistant to the (US) President for Economic Policy, most Airbnb renters are from the working class people. These renters rent out their master bedroom to travelers for about 66 days per year. This generates, approximately, an additional $7350 in annual income for a middle-class family, equivalent to a 14% increase. According to statistics from Airbnb, homeowners in San Francisco rent out their master bedrooms for 58 days on average each year, which earns them a total of USD 9300.

According to the *State of the Sharing Economy Report 2013* published on the website of The People Who Share, British participants in the sharing economy gain an additional income of £416.16 per year. Some gain as much as £5000. American participants in the sharing economy gained additional income totaling $3.5 billion in 2013, a year-on-year increase of 25%.

According to a survey by well-known car rental platform RelayRides, the average private car owner who rents out their car through this platform earns USD 250 per month. Some car owners have even earned enough to cover the cost of their vehicle.

According to *Unlocking the Sharing Economy*, an independent report released by the UK Office of Government Commerce, there are more than 20,000 people in the UK who rent out their parking spaces through JustPark, earning an additional income of £465 per year on average (£810 in London). Those who rent out their cars through easyCar Club can earn £1800 per year.

While there is no official data in China showing that the sharing economy boosts residents' income, the representative platforms in several fields allows us to make certain observations.

According to statistics from surveys by Didi Chuxing, 96.5% of the drivers have seen increases in their monthly income (to varying degrees) after they began to offer ride-hailing services. 78.1% of drivers have seen their incomes increase by more than 10%, while 39.5% of drivers have seen their incomes increase by more than 30%. Yang Feng (pseudonym), a Didi driver, said on December 30, 2015 that he received more than 2000 ride-hailing requests over the past few months, which generated quite a respectable income after subsidies from Didi. Yang Feng also added that he operates his own restaurant—Didi is only part-time work for him. "Previously, I was driving a Kia K2 before I switched to this Passat. I footed the down payment for my new car using my earnings as a Didi driver over these few months."

On the Zaihang platform launched by guokr.com, users spend 200 to 500 yuan per hour on consultations for questions they may have in such areas as the internet, financial investments, and education. Assuming that, on average, an "industry expert" provides 10 h of consulting services per month, they can boost their monthly income by 2000 to 5000 yuan. According to statistics on the number of experts on the Zaihang website, there are roughly 8000 experts active on this platform, 56% of whom live in Beijing. As of February 29, 2016, Zhuge Siyuan had the greatest number of successful appointments—she has provided 645 one-on-one in-person consultations at 499 yuan per session, generating an income of over 300,000 yuan.

Let us now return to the "private kitchen" platforms, chiefly represented by Go Home To Eat, Good Chef, Xiaoeguanfan, Mother's Dishes, and Cengfan. More than 500 chefs are registered on the Good Chef platform. Meanwhile, Zhou Tong, the director of operations at Go Home to Eat, has said that "over 1000 people from hundreds of residential communities in Beijing work part-time by cooking in their own kitchens". According to the current uniform pricing standards on Good Chef platform, a meal of six dishes and one soup costs 99 yuan, while four dishes and one soup cost 79 yuan, provided that the ingredients are provided by the user. Assuming that a part-time chef cooks 4 to 6 courses per day, they can increase their monthly income by roughly 2000 yuan. According to *Legal Weekly*, Zhang Li (pseudonym), who is a full-time housewife, has found part-time work online. Zhang says that she can now prepare takeaway dishes when preparing meals for her family, which is much like earning extra income from a part-time job.

New Sources of Consumption Growth

China is advocating the cultivation of new growth areas with regards to consumption, as well as the boosting of economic growth through exports, consumption and investment. As downward economic pressures intensify, stimulating domestic demand will become a pivotal means for managing downward pressures on the economy.

The sharing economy offers new possibilities for China's efforts to adjust its economic structure and transform the drivers of economic growth. Compared to traditional forms of industry, the sharing economy stimulates economic growth without the need for additional investment. What the sharing economy does is to rationally redistribute existing resources, allowing society to operate more efficiently through the optimal allocation of supply (products and services) and demand.

The American Action Forum drew an important conclusion from the research report *Independent Contractors and the Emerging Gig Economy*: Despite its infancy, the sharing economy will become an important source of growth for the American economy in the twenty-first century.

Similarly, the sharing economy will be an important source of growth for China's economy. Take short-term rentals for instance. According to the *China Research Report on Online Vacation and Rental Market 2016* by iResearch and the *China Report on the C2C Model of Online Vacation and Rental Market 2016* by Analysys, transactions on China's online vacation and rental market reached approximately 4.26 billion yuan in 2015, a year-on-year increase of 122.0%. According to iResearch, outbound tourism will generate rapid growth in the market for outbound vacation rentals from the second half of 2016 to 2017. In 2017, transactions across China's online market for vacation rentals are expected to reach a scale of 10.3 billion yuan.

According to the *Domestic Travel and Short-term Rental Trend Development Report 2015* released by mayi.com and Sogou Big Data in January 2016, domestic tourism exceeded 4 billion in 2015, meaning that the average Chinese citizen travelled more than 3 times a year. Meanwhile, figures from the mayi.com platform show that up to 80% of its users are tourists. Most users who choose short-term rentals are travelers.

The report also shows that the predictions made by iResearch, Sootoo Research Institute, Analysys, etc.—namely that the size of the domestic market for short-term rentals will see a year-on-year increase of 163.0%, and is expected to exceed 10 billion yuan in 2015—seem to be somewhat conservative.

As the market for short-term rentals expands, it is certain that short-term rentals will become a new source of growth for consumption in China.

As for commuting, the scale of the market for car rentals continues to grow. A report by Roland Berger Consulting pointed out that the market for car rentals in China was 34 billion yuan in 2013, and will grow to 65 billion yuan in 2018.

As for platforms for trading second-hand goods, Xianyu has a market capitalization upwards of USD 3 billion. According to official data from Xianyu, more than 200,000 idle products successfully change hands each day on the platform. The Xianyu platform mainly facilitates the trade of second-hand items of a certain value, such as digital products, sports equipment, clothes, and shoes. Assuming that the average item costs 100 yuan, daily turnover would be 20 million yuan, monthly turnover would be 600 million yuan, while annual turnover would be 7.2 billion yuan.

Zhuanzhuan, also a trading platform for idle products, which operates under the slogan "Save 5.6-million-yuan worth of idle products each day", has an annual turnover of up to 2 billion yuan.

Sales at Beijing Xidan JOY CITY, an ordinary shopping mall, reached 2.049 billion yuan in the first half of 2015. A comparison of the two shows that the size of the market for second-hand goods is not to be sneezed at.

Some may wonder why there is greater potential for the sharing economy to drive economic growth, given that the traditional economy sees greater consumption of new products corresponding to these needs?

In our view, much consumer demand is greatly suppressed due to prices that are unduly high. Take short-term rentals for instance. Not everyone can afford a hotel room. Yet, short-term rentals have met the needs of more people. People may now own or use the products and services that they require at a lower price. When such "suppressed" demand is released, total consumption will increase accordingly.

CHAPTER 12

Employment Opportunities

According to the Central Economic Work Conference, resolving the problem of excess production capacity is the greatest of the five major tasks facing supply-side structural reforms in 2016. This involves the orderly exit of "zombie enterprises" from the market. Factors such as the reorganization of SOEs and the withdrawal of zombie enterprises from the market will inevitably put great pressure on employment in China.

The sharing economy can create diverse channels and opportunities for employment. The "rise of roles" has created new employment opportunities and relieved downwards pressures on employment. Note, this refers to employment opportunities, not actual job positions. Employment opportunities are of a temporary nature, where there may be no formal contract between employer and employee. This manifests as an "occupational identity". In contrast, job positions are fixed, where there are clear distinctions between the roles of employer and employee. In general, these involve signed employment agreements.

Americans have greater experience in this regard, and exhibit an optimism that is more "radical". James Altucher, a well-known American venture capital fund manager, is an interesting case in point. Altucher has many "occupational identities", being the founder or co-founder of over 20 companies, in addition to writing books and articles. He is also active on Podcast.

In a recently published post, *10 Reasons You Have To Quit Your Job in 2016*, James gives a caution to office workers: It is time for white-collar

M. Huateng et al., *The Chinese Sharing Economy*,
https://doi.org/10.1007/978-981-33-6494-3_12

workers who receive a fixed salary to say goodbye to 9 to 5 work and become a professional freelancer on the internet. According to the article, the "Excess Capacity" economy will only continue to grow. There are many platforms available for selection, including Airbnb and Uber, as well as Alibaba, eBay, Etsy, and Infusionsoft, to name but a few. Therefore, to take advantage of opportunity ahead of time, you should take stock of yourself and your surroundings and see what valuables can be traded in in the market. We say "take stock of yourself" because your intellectual "wealth" is also an asset. Never underestimate your brainpower. We are living in an "idea economy", where we can become a creative worker at any time.

The Next Big Thing

Ron Conway and Esther Dyson, two well-known angel investors in Silicon Valley, as well as John Hennessy, president of Stanford University, discussed the impact of the sharing economy on employees and entrepreneurs at The Next Big Thing Conference held in 2014 by Bloomberg. Conway and Dyson believe that enterprises such as Uber and Airbnb are creating jobs, and that the sharing economy has the potential to alter the rules of the game. Before robots take over certain jobs, humans will still be required.

After interviewing 778 people in December 2013, researchers from Boston University found that the income they earned from "non-regular work" during their leisure time was equivalent to, on average, 4.4% of their regular income. Even after excluding income from selling things or renting out rooms, their "non-regular" income was 1.8% of their employment income.

As mentioned earlier, the sharing economy is sometimes called the "gig economy". According to the research report *Independent Contractors and the Emerging Gig Economy* released by the American Action Forum, from 2002 to 2014, the increase in the number of Americans engaged in the gig economy was somewhere between 8.8% to 14.4%, whereas overall employment in the United States increased by only 7.2% over the same period. In particular, the online sharing economy grew at a rapid rate, especially the transport and accommodation sectors, chiefly represented by Uber and Airbnb. For example, from 2009 to 2013, the ridesharing industry contributed USD 519 million to the American economy and created 22,000 jobs.

It is obvious that the sharing economy has given rise to a new social division of labor and altered traditional models of employment. People now enjoy a measure of flexibility in their choice of employment, based on their interests and skills, and engage in economic activities as self-employed workers without relying on companies. This has prompted more people to work on a freelance basis, making the importance of employment opportunities increasingly obvious.

From the perspective of crowdsourcing logistics, as the end of July 2015, rrkd.cn platform has over twelve million members, nearly ten million of whom are freelance deliverymen. Tens of thousands of orders are processed on the platform every day. Dada, another logistics platform, which operates in over 40 cities including Beijing, Shanghai, and Guangzhou, serves more than 150,000 merchants and processes 1 million orders per day. On December 31, 2015, Dada completed its "Series D" round of financing, which raised about $300 million in capital. With a valuation of over $1 billion, the platform has become a new unicorn.

According to data provided by zbj.com, the platform brings together 3 million micro-enterprises and 11 million cultural and creative talents in creative design, marketing planning, and technology development, as well as service talents who offer business, decoration, and life services. Weike, another part-time service platform, boasts over 8 million technical professionals.

In the car sharing market, the *Monitoring Report on the Car Sharing Market in the Third Quarter of 2015* released by Analysys shows that four companies, Didi Hitch, Dida Pinche, Tiantian Yongche and 51 Yongche, occupy 98.2% of the market. Didi Hitch has 5.5 million drivers, occupying about 69.0% of the market, while Dida Pinche has 1.5 million certified drivers, with a market share of 20.9%. Based on this, the number of participants in the car sharing market is estimated at about 8 million.

The sharing economy can create jobs for persons whose previous jobs have been made redundant by industrial upgrading, whether they were previously engaged in work that required mental effort or physical effort. Without cumbersome procedures and with a low employment threshold, participants can share idle resources across society and earn a reasonable income from online sharing platforms.

At the same time, when professional freelancers, sole proprietors, and other individuals engage in part-time work or outsource services through the various sharing economy platforms, labor contracts are no longer a prerequisite for employment. Short-term labor relations have become the mainstream in the emerging employment market.

The McKinsey report published in June 2015 also showed that, globally, over 200 million people with various skills are able to work for longer hours and earn a greater income from freelance work platforms. Part-time work on a large scale has become a trend.

Self-Employed Persons and Prosumers

From an economic perspective, there are many overlapping aspects between the self-employed economy and the sharing economy. However, the former focuses on labor relations while the latter on the description of business models.

There is a huge number of self-employed persons in China. The Chinese Academy of Social Sciences stated in the article "Social groups and income inequality in China" that the self-employed population accounts for some 11.51% of the total employed population in China, and their monthly income accounts for 13.89% of total earned income. They are regarded as a key component of the "old middle class". Based on a total employed population of some 760 million, there are 87 million self-employed people. The *zigu jieceng* (literally "self-employed class"[1]) is a novel expression that has emerged over the course of urbanization, whose members were originally from rural regions or the "urban underclass". Most are unskilled workers unable to seek employment at enterprises and public institutions. Many of them operate self-employed businesses or "family-style workshops" and are "low-level" proprietors with a bit of capital or owners of small family businesses who are unable or unwilling to work at enterprises.

The term "self-employed [persons]" is usually translated as *ziyou zhiye zhe* (freelancers, persons in "free" employment[2]) in the Chinese Mainland a. According to the *Reading Guide on the Report of the 16th National*

[1] This does not refer to "class" in the traditional sense of the word, but rather a group of people characterized by the nature of their employment, i.e. a "self-employed social group".

[2] *ziyou zhiye zhe* is usually translated as freelancer. However, *ziyou zhiye zhe* is somewhat broader than "freelancer" in the strict sense, as it may include owners of (unregistered) small businesses. The term is best understood as encompassing all working persons who are not subject to traditional work structures. However, for most intents and purposes, the term "freelancer" is adequate.

Congress of the Communist Party of China: "Before the founding of the People's Republic of China, '*ziyou zhiye zhe*' generally refers to doctors, teachers, lawyers, journalists, authors, artists, and so on, who harness their knowledge and skills to make an independent living. Today, the term refers to those workers who do not have formal labor relations with an employer, but who are not sole proprietors or owners of private businesses. These workers have a measure of "economic power",[3] professional knowledge and know-how, and provide lawful services to society."

The term "prosumer" refers to a person who is both producer and consumer. In the sharing economy, consumers play the roles of both supplier and consumer when participating in sharing economy platforms like Uber and Airbnb. Therefore, self-employed workers are indistinguishable from prosumers.

In the US, the self-employed economy emerged at a time of economic downturn. Following the economic crisis in 2008, a great many American companies, regardless of size, were forced to shut down or lay off workers, causing the unemployment rate to soar to 10%, which was a huge issue for the Obama administration. In contrast, however, the number of self-employed people rose sharply. *China Securities Journal* reported that one out of every 3 workers in the US works on a freelance basis, across all sorts of industries, including software engineers, those in the art industry, and salesmen. There were 42 million freelancers in the US at the time of the report, a threefold increase over 2005. "The US is moving towards an era of professional freelancers," *Forbes* announced on its Chinese website. MBO Partners, a recruitment agency, predicts that before 2020, the number of freelancers and independent workers in the USA will soar to 65 million. Professional freelancers, who were on the fringes of society, are increasingly becoming an economic force that cannot be ignored in the USA. Some have even called the "professional freelancer economy" the industrial revolution of this era.

In Japan, an aging society has spurred the development of the self-employed economy. According to statistics released by the Japanese Ministry of Internal Affairs and Communications, professional freelancers accounted for 6.8%—a record high—of the young labor force in Japan in 2013. There were 1.82 million professional freelancers who worked on a part-time basis. Japanese analysts have concluded that population ageing

[3] That is, financial means.

in Japan will continue to worsen. There will be even fewer young Japanese in the future, given changing attitudes towards childbirth. Instead of seeking formal, stable employment, many young people opt to work on a short-term, part-time or temporary basis. The large number of young people engaged in these forms of employment has greatly increased the proportion of freelancers in the labor force.

China's economic development has now reached a "new normal", where GDP is projected to grow at a "medium-high rate" instead of the breakneck pace of the past. Based on the experience of developed countries, this figure may even be further reduced in the future. As Chinese society ages, there will be changes to the attitudes of young people towards employment, and the number of professional internet freelancers will grow, causing this tendency to become more and more pronounced.

The main players in the "freelancer market" are Upwork in the USA and Freelancer.com in Australia, both of whom have completed multiple rounds of financing.

"There are about 230 million knowledge workers in the world, and the global freelance market will grow to a size of USD 2 trillion to USD 3 trillion in the future," according to Fabio Rosati, a member of Upwork's board. LinkedIn, a professional social platform, has also begun to harness its platform and resource advantages to gain a slice of the "sharing economy pie" by connecting more freelancers with job opportunities.

Practical Significance

"Internet Plus Self-Employment" is of great significance to China's economy and society.

First, Job Creation

In the 1990s, SOE reforms led to the retrenchment of tens of millions of employees. In 2008, employment opportunities in cities were in the doldrums due to the global financial crisis, forcing over 12 million rural migrant workers to return to their hometowns. In recent years, some industries, such as iron & steel and coal, have begun downsize as a result of excess production capacity. As technology progresses in leaps and bounds, some repetitive jobs have been replaced by robots.

Recently, Zeng Xiangquan, director of the China Institute for Employment Research, has indicated that China should be ready for a second wave of layoffs arising from factors such as the reorganization of SOEs. The 2015 Q3 "hiring index" released by China International Intellectech, a state-owned enterprise, was minus 0.79%, a significant year-on-year decrease.

Regarding media reports of layoffs, Yin Weimin, Minister of Human Resources and Social Security, said that there have been no "large-scale layoffs" by enterprises. At the same time, Yin indicated frankly that the total labor force remains large. On the one hand, enterprises have experiencing difficulties in recruitment; on the other hand, people are finding it difficult to find jobs. As "front-line" service jobs are highly labor-intensive but command low wages, they are not attractive to new-generation migrant workers, which have caused difficulties in recruitment. Meanwhile, the entry of over 7 million university graduates into the job market have created a shortage of jobs. It is estimated that, over the period of the 13th Five-Year Plan period, there will be 25 million people hunting for jobs each year, causing great pressure on employment.

As far as society is concerned, the self-employed economy can ease employment pressure and revitalize traditional industries through innovation. Becoming self-employed also contributes to the job market—employment pressures in China will be greatly eased if more people are willing to undertake self-employment.

As we know, economic growth is a barometer for employment. In recent years, China's economy faces a grim test of simultaneously dealing with the slowdown in economic growth, making difficult structural adjustments, and absorbing the effects of previous economic stimulus policies. GDP growth is transitioning from a phase of rapid growth to a phase of medium-high growth, even as more people seek employment. Slower growth has brought pressure to employment growth.

The self-employed economy has allowed us to understand innovation and entrepreneurship from another perspective. We have found that imbalances between supply and demand in traditional industries has vanished. Regardless of whether their jobs require mental effort or physical effort, workers are now able to easily share idle resources on online sharing platforms and thereby generate a reasonable income.

According to a special survey conducted by Peking University School of New Media, Didi Chuxing has created over 200,600 jobs, both directly and indirectly, through ride-hailing services.

Through online sharing platforms, self-employed workers have gained "invisible employment", which effectively supplements traditional "visible" employment relations. The self-employed sector has undoubtedly stabilized the employment market even as the economy faces headwinds.

Second, Industry Innovation

From the perspective of industry competition, "Internet Plus Self-Employment" also helps to revitalize traditional industries.

Traditional industries face a dilemma. It is hard for the increasingly ossified market system to meet growing market demand. For example, given existing supply capacity and administrative management models, urban transport falls far short of meeting the enormous demand from consumers. This even gives rise to a gray area—a huge market for unlicensed taxis.

The self-employed economy helps resolve such contradictions. By directly linking self-employed workers and consumers, sharing platforms remove the existing constraints on companies and companies, bring into play untapped idle productivity, and stimulate market innovation through a market model akin to perfect competition. While bringing diversity, convenience and economic benefits to consumers, these platforms also promote the transformation and upgrading of traditional industries. As a result, breakthroughs have been made in areas such as the reform of the taxi industry and the rent-to-own model for traditional car makers.

Despite being hailed as the world's largest taxi company, Uber does not own a single car. Founded nearly one hundred years ago, Hilton, a hotel giant, has only 715,000 rooms across the world. Meanwhile, up to 1 million rooms have been registered and shared on the Airbnb platform since its founding in 2008.

On the one hand, the strengths of such innovations lie in the asset-light operations of the companies behind sharing platforms. These companies are free of cost constraints when coordinating suppliers without cost constraints. They are able to achieve large-scale development rapidly as their broad supply base allows them to meet the highly diversified needs of users. On the other hand, a particularly significant aspect is that platform companies only pay for the services actually offered by self-employed workers. They are not required to bear extra insurance and welfare expenses. Compared to asset-heavy enterprises in the same business sector, these platforms enjoy a better yield on investment, making their business model popular in the capital markets. Figures show that Uber and Airbnb rank among the top three global startups with a value of USD 1 billion or more.

Third, Virtual Enterprises

From the perspective of the self-employed economy, the traditional "full-time workers, on-site work" model is antiquated, and has been replaced by more flexible forms of corporate organization. Companies are now able to break free of geographical, industry, and professional constraints to attract the professionals that they require in a more flexible manner, thus transitioning towards the "virtual enterprise" mode of operations.

This allows a company to tap on richer human resources. Operating under such models as outsourcing and crowdsourcing, companies can more efficiently match supply and demand during market peaks and troughs, and develop a more balanced corporate labor structure. For example, Wonolo provides on-demand loading and unloading services for retailers, helping them flexibly allocate manpower. A similar platform, Zaaly, provides temporary manpower services for enterprises.

It is no longer the case that enterprises are served only by full-time employees. Many consultant-type "external brains" are also required, which can help enterprises acquire better resources, especially in the field of cultural and creative services. For instance, various "Witkey" platforms provide professional service transactions for enterprises and individuals alike.

Two Challenges

The self-employed economy poses some challenges to society, among which two aspects have attracted the greatest controversy. One is the risk to the social security system caused by the self-employment model, while the other is the issue of trust on sharing platforms.

First, Without a Social Safety Net, a Cost Crisis Lurks Behind Freelance Work

In a self-employed economy, sharing platforms and participating suppliers are independent contractors. Platforms are exempt from performing the obligations required of an employer. Independent contractors are self-employed without the social security inherent in the traditional employment model, such as retirement insurance, unemployment insurance, work injury insurance, health insurance, pensions, overtime pay, maternity leave, etc. It is difficult to ensure workers' rights in the event of labor disputes, such as work-related injuries. If freelance work develops on a large scale in the absence of social security mechanisms, it is possible that the social security system, which underlies the social safety net, may fail entirely.

For part-time workers who work on the sideline, it is difficult to define whether labor disputes should be handled according to the rules for regular or part-time jobs. Self-employed workers who do full-time work on platforms are gradually coming to realize that remuneration is not equal to work. For example, despite being an intermediary, platforms still impose many administrative requirements on self-employed workers, prompting a great deal of related lawsuits. For example, Uber and Lyft in the ride-hailing sector, Homejoy in the housekeeping service sector, and Instacart in the crowdsourcing logistics sector have found themselves facing lawsuits. According to current figures, if the self-employment model is no longer recognized, young sharing platforms will have to bear an increase of 30% or more in social security expenses for self-employed workers. This will undoubtedly make it harder for startups to grow.

In addition to the challenges of safeguarding the rights and interests of suppliers directly linked to platforms, demands related to consumers' interests are also one of the issues that self-employed platforms must concentrate on. According to media reports, in January 2016, a university student in Nanjing surnamed Chen met with an accident while using Didi's Hitch service, but the insurance company rejected the claim on the grounds that the vehicle was not authorized for commercial use. It turned out that the passenger Chen, who often uses Didi's Hitch service, was injured when the driver, surnamed Liu, collided with another car while swerving to avoid a third vehicle. Liu and Chen hoped for compensation from the insurance company. However, after learning that the accident occurred when the vehicle was operating as a "ride-hailing vehicle", the insurance company held that Liu's vehicle was insured as a private car, and that Liu had changed the usage of his vehicle, which increased the vehicle risk, without seeking authorization. The insurer therefore rejected the claim. Liu also hit a wall when he turned to Didi for assistance.

Ultimately, the passenger and the owner reached a compensation agreement with assistance from the police. But it is noteworthy that neither party received insurance compensation, whether from Liu's private car insurer or Didi's insurers. This is just one of the myriad cases in which there are loopholes in the self-employed economy with regards to the protection of the rights of employees and users. Though the sharing economy is still in its infancy, similar incidents have cropped up all over the world. As the self-employed economy continues to face greater scrutiny, there will be greater doubts about and increased demands on these platforms and companies, making it an issue urgently in need of a solution.

Second, Loose Management Models Give Rise to Trust Issues, Compromising the Long-Term Development of Sharing Platforms

Sharing platforms have expanded "the scope of sharing" from "strong social circles" to between strangers that are only "weakly related'. As trust is a prerequisite for sharing, a "trust guarantee system" determines the degree of trust, which in turn influences sharing activities and the development of platforms. Suppliers on sharing platforms are self-employed workers, with a "loose management relationship" with the platform. On the one hand, it is difficult for platforms to manage self-employed workers, who constitute an unstable workforce. At the same time, self-employed workers hail from diverse backgrounds and vary in quality. When rapidly expanding, platforms find it hard to ensure the quality of customer-oriented services, creating a host of trust issues, such as security problems and poor user experiences. Therefore, a platform needs to provide handsome subsidies to maintain the "stickiness" of suppliers and users, while resorting to various administrative rules to avoid and remedy these issues after the fact.

The importance of trust in the development of the sharing economy is analyzed in other parts of this book. Trust is also one of the key issues faced by the sharing economy. An increasing number of sharing platforms are trying to build a sound "trust guarantee system". However, it has to be recognized that there is still a long way to go, and this requires joint efforts by sharing platforms in conjunction with legal oversight and the general public.

CHAPTER 13

Environmental Protection

Achieving a moderately prosperous society in all respects and improving the ecological environment are historical tasks for China. These have created unprecedented development opportunities for the environmental sector, while also demanding more of its capabilities and standards. Many hold the view that a relationship of harmonious progress exists between environmental protection and the economic model of the sharing economy. For example, Sajid Javid, the British Secretary of State for Business, has argued that, through more efficient resource utilization, the sharing economy has had a positive influence on the environment. Moreover, in *A Market Definition Report: The Collaborative Economy*, Jeremian Owyang also lists environmental pressures as one of the societal forces driving the sharing economy.

What is the relationship between the sharing economy and environmental protection? It can be summed up in three respects: First, slower consumption of resources. Second, lower pollution levels. Third, promoting environmental protection.

As mentioned above, the sharing economy can achieve the repeated and efficient use of exploited resources by redistributing existing resources. This slows down resource exploitation to a certain degree.

M. Huateng et al., *The Chinese Sharing Economy*,
https://doi.org/10.1007/978-981-33-6494-3_13

Slower Resource Exploitation

"Resources" can be divided into natural resources and "social resources". Not all natural resources are inexhaustible. A case in point is mineral resources, reserves of which are depleted whenever exploited, although some can be recycled or reused. The impact of resource consumption on the environment is twofold. First, natural resources are part of the environment, and the loss of environmental value caused by the exhaustion of natural resources is irreversible. Second, if the process of resource depletion exceeds the ecosystem's restorative capacity, the ecological equilibrium will be upset, causing a deterioration in the living environment for human beings, such as the occurrence of catastrophic floods and sandstorms.

As we can imagine, if you buy a second-hand wooden chair instead of a new one, it will reduce the consumption of timber. If more people follow suit, it will slow down deforestation, making it possible for the ecosystem to regulate itself, thus benefitting environmental conservation efforts.

In addition to wood, there are all sorts of other minerals, as well as water, oil, animals, and so on. Andre Veneman, director of AkzoNobel Global Sustainability and HSE, has said that, "With dwindling resources, people should adopt a completely different mindset, and seek a new circular approach in solving this problem. We need to be aware of the potential value of each material. This is not only corporate social responsibility, but also business acumen." The business models of the sharing economy show that people have adopted a different mindset when examining the potential value of goods.

Extending the "Use Time" of Items

Of the three basic business models of the sharing economy, the second-hand trading market can best reflect the impact of the sharing economy on resource utilization. When a second-hand product is reused through sharing, the "use time" of items (that is, increasing the instances where a resource is utilized and achieving its repeated utilization) and the "use value" (increasing the value of resources, i.e. the efficient utilization of resources) are extended. We can systematically avoid and reduce waste in the course of economic activities, and leave behind the "hell-bent production and consumption" of the traditional industrial economy. The online second-hand trading market is booming, indicating that a wealth of idle items has been once again put into use. For example, second-hand sales in the US account for some 10% of the overall online shopping market. In China, the number of online second-hand trading platforms is growing, including the well-known "Zhuanzhuan" under 58.com and second-hand platform "Xianyu" under Taobao. At the same time, more and more people are becoming active users of online second-hand trading platforms. For example, "Zhuanzhuan" was launched on the second day of the 2015 "Double Eleven" (Singles' Day) Festival. According to official data from "Zhuanzhuan", more than 9,000 idle products were put on sale by nearly 110,000 users on "Zhuanzhuan" on its first day, resulting in 1,137 orders. "Xianyu" has also been developing rapidly in recent years. "Xianyu" has a large number of users, since Taobao members are not required to register before using the platform. According to official data from the platform, over 200,000 idle items are traded on "Xianyu" each day. Consumers and operators speak of the platform in glowing terms. Given the successful trading of second-hand in the sharing economy, idle goods have become high-quality consumer goods for reuse rather than being consigned to the scrapyard. This is equivalent to extending consumers' use of products, thus cutting waste and excessive consumption.

Reducing the Consumption of Resources

Take, for instance, Didi Chuxing. The company's business models for services, such as Didi "Kuaiche", Didi Hitch, carpooling, car rental, and coaches also reduce the consumption of energy resources such as gasoline.

Studies conducted by *The Economist* magazine have concluded that "one extra car in a car-sharing service typically takes 9-13 cars off the road", and can even cut the mileage of the "sharers" by 44%. According to research by Massachusetts Institute of Technology (MIT), UberPool, a car sharing service, can reduce traffic congestion by 55% and the number of taxis by 40%. Moreover, Sunil Paul, CEO of SideCar, pointed out that: "There's this idea that owning a car gives you freedom, but freedom is being able to get where you want. And with [innovation], you don't need to own a car to do that. Within 10 years, I think car ownership will be cut in half."

As can be seen from the figures above, the sharing economy can reduce per capita energy consumption and car ownership. On the one hand, the number of vehicles produced will be reduced, thereby curtailing the consumption of resources required to make new cars. On the other hand, a reduction in car ownership also means less congestion and less traffic on highways—traffic congestion consumes large amounts of energy. In this respect, the sharing economy also reduces resource consumption.

Lower Levels of Pollution

In contrast with the two points above, it is hard to quantity the complex relationship between the sharing economy and pollution levels. Some areas where the sharing economy is popular, such as finance, culture and entertainment, have little impact on pollution levels. However, services for residents may increase transport required for the greater circulation of goods and services, resulting in greater pollution levels. Compared to other sectors, the development of housing and car sharing may have a more direct impact on pollution levels.

First, relevant studies show that compared to traditional hotels, "shared houses" can cut carbon emissions per capita. Due to smaller public areas and lower demand for energy, tenants in family residences consume less energy. Airbnb revealed a survey report compiled by Cleantech Group, an environmental consulting group, in its blog post *A Greener Way to Travel: The Environmental Impacts of Home Sharing*. In 2013, Cleantech conducted a questionnaire survey that involved 8,000 tenants and landlords from all over the world. The data shows that European tenants who stay in a house provided by Airbnb for one night emitted 89% less greenhouse gases compared to those staying in hotels. The equivalent figure In North America is as high as 61%. In terms of total emissions, the reduction in emissions attributed to Airbnb in Europe and North America are respectively equivalent to greenhouse gas emissions from 200,000 and 33,000 cars. This report also shows that Airbnb has reduced the quantity of energy and water used by customers. The environmental protection effect is patently obvious.

Second, shared cars can reduce pollution levels caused by traffic congestion in cities. Car sharing lowers the per capita use of cars and reduces road traffic. At the same time, fewer required parking spaces make room for urban greening. According to the results of research conducted by the government of Germany's City Municipality of Bremen, for each additional car shared results in 11 fewer private cars. The data also shows that 50% of people owned one vehicle before joining car sharing, but about 37.1% abandoned private cars after joining car sharing. According to the latest report *What's Ahead for Car Sharing: The New Mobility and Its Impact on Vehicle Sales* released by Boston Consulting Group in February 2016, car sales are expected to fall by about 5% in 2021 due to car sharing. The growth rate of China's car market is expected to fall from 11% to about 5% by 2025. Therefore, from the perspective of traffic congestion, the sharing economy exerts a positive effect on emissions reductions.

Third, in terms of production, the car manufacturing sector is one of the heavy industries and a high energy consumption and high pollution sector. The development of the second-hand car market and car sharing will also reduce the output of new cars and the resulting pollution. In early 2016, China Passenger Car Association released the 2015 Ranking of Automobile Sales in China, which showed that the sales of passenger cars (broadly defined) totaled 20.58 million. According to *Sohu Automobile Report on 2015 China Second-hand Car Trading Data Analysis*, in 2015, China's overall second-hand car trading (independent VIN) reached 7,047,400 vehicles, and the actual number of vehicles transferred surpassed 9.6 million. This comparison shows that second-hand car transactions accounted for some 1/3 of total vehicle transactions in 2015.

However, there is no denying that, all things being equal, second-hand cars may consume more fuel and generate more pollution than new cars. Therefore, the pollution caused by the rise of the second-hand car market needs to be evaluated from multiple perspectives.

Fourth, in terms of consumption, the impact of a sharing economy model on consumer demand is complicated. The "rise" of second-hand products may replace consumer demand for new products to a certain extent. This effect may be transmitted to production, thereby reducing the output of new products and production-related pollution. At the same time, however, the sharing economy may also stimulate consumer demand in other areas, or spur product innovation, and stimulating production by increasing the updating of products. Moreover, new demand may necessitate the transport of goods and services, resulting in increased pollution. At present, it is hard to draw a convincing conclusion as to whether the booming sharing economy contributes to emissions reductions.

Promoting Environmental Protection

The Chinese government attaches great importance to supply-side reform, and has promulgated favorable policies. For companies in the environmental sector, the key is to find a solution to free themselves from serving companies with excess production capacity and find their own path towards industrial transformation and upgrading. "Sharing economy" concepts are gaining popularity, providing a new direction for the development of the environmental industry.

First, the sharing economy has been adopted in the electricity sector. For example, each home becomes a small power station through a home photovoltaic or wind power system, sharing surplus electricity on the power grid. Germany has already begun test runs in this area, where a great many households use green energy (solar energy, wind energy, etc.) to generate electricity, selling surplus electricity to other households or the state. Jeremy Rifkin, an economist and futurist, has said that this has allowed large German electricity producers to cut total electricity output across the country by 7%. Power generation by large power producers (mostly thermal power generation, nuclear power generation, etc.) are not as environmentally friendly as these dispersed family-run power stations (almost no pollutants are emitted when generating electricity from new energy sources). Therefore, these small power plants bring benefits to residents, and also lower environmental pollution. This model has therefore been popularized in Germany.

Secondly, environmentally-friendly means of travel such as new energy vehicles and bicycles can develop rapidly with support from the sharing economy. In 2015, eHi Car Services also announced that the launch of new-energy vehicle rental services, where users could rent the Brilliance BMW Zinoro 1E in Beijing, and the Roewe 550 Plug-in in Shanghai. In future, such services may be extended to other cities. GreenGo Car Rental launched electric vehicle sharing services in Beijing that feature easy charging and affordable prices. Eakay new energy vehicle sharing cloud platform has also launches hourly-based new energy vehicle rental services. These models of travel have cut pollution emissions while promoting environmental protection in local areas.

Mr. Li, an employee of an internet company, enjoys the benefits that the sharing economy brings to daily life. Previously, he commuted to work by bus or taxi (which was expensive). Mr. Li now can enjoy convenient and inexpensive Didi rides. He used to worry about what to have for dinner after work, but can now enjoy a meal from the Go Home to Eat app when he reaches home, as long as he places his order before the end of the workday. Having benefited from the sharing economy, Mr. Li is also eager to become a part of the "sharers". He is applying for a "new-energy vehicle license plate", and intends to become a Didi Hitch driver, which would earn him extra income while bringing convenience to others.

Ofo bike sharing is attracting the attention of university students in Beijing. Of the more than 5,000 "little yellow bikes", apart from the vehicles provided by the platform, students share their own idle bikes, which have been painted and retrofitted by the platform operator. As shared bicycles offer greater freedom of movement without the need to undertake the costs of maintenance and repair, many students share idle bicycles on the platform, allowing Ofo to develop rapidly in a short time. The number of shared bicycles on the platform soared from 2,000 to over 5,000 within six months. Bicycle sharing greatly increases the usage frequency of idle bicycles, and also reduces travel costs for students. As information sharing and environmentally friendly mobility gain popularity in universities, commercial bike sharing platforms such as Ofo will enjoy greater room for development.

PART IV

Transformation: Marching Towards the New Economy

CHAPTER 14

Declaration of Sharism

The sharing economy is shaking the foundations of traditional sectors based on the exchange of goods and services. We no longer see ownership as the best way to acquire products. Instead of focusing on buying and owning products or services, we have adopted a mindset of cooperation and sharing, and are more inclined to acquire products or services on a temporary basis or share them with others.

If you look at the current "sharing economy" mindset from this standpoint, it becomes not a question of how much you give me, but rather how we cooperate and share. The fundamental concepts of traditional economics are no longer valid.

As Umair Haque, author of *The New Capitalist Manifesto*, put it, "If the people formerly known as consumers begin consuming 10% less and peering 10% more, the effect on margins of traditional corporations is going to be disproportionately greater, which means certain industries have to rewire themselves, or prepare to sink into the quicksand of the past."

This prediction by Umair Haque, which was once merely a source of worry for traditional enterprises, has become a reality. The butterfly effect of the sharing economy is "brewing". According to a 2015 survey of global corporate executives by IBM, senior executives believe that Uber-style game-changing intrusions pose the biggest imminent threat to competition, and that the boundaries of competition are becoming increasingly blurred.

M. Huateng et al., *The Chinese Sharing Economy*,
https://doi.org/10.1007/978-981-33-6494-3_14

IBM's research report points out that Judy Lemke, Chief Information Officer at Schneider, believes that "This is the 'Uber syndrome'. Competitors join the industry with a wholly different business model. You find yourself powerless in the face of this." Ian Cunningham, Chief Operating Officer at Tangerine Bank, has said, "It is hard to predict the ever-changing technological climate. You are not aware of what knowledge you require, but you still have to strive to take the lead." For the global executives involved in the survey, the biggest threat comes from new competitors not yet regarded as competitors.

For traditional industries, the sharing economy brings tremendous opportunities. Although established business models and sources of income are undermined by the rise of enterprises which adopt the sharing economy, the sharing economy also provides enterprises with a wealth of transformation opportunities and channels of potential profit that would allow them to transition towards this more sustainable consumption model.

In the face of the sharing economy, how should traditional industries follow suit and embrace the resulting market benefits? Leading enterprises have played an exemplary role in this respect. Here, we shall summarize and dissect the measures taken by representative enterprises, in order to provide lessons for enterprises seeking to make breakthroughs in the sharing economy.

First, Embrace

Traditional enterprises can actively embrace the sharing economy by launching related products and services, shifting from selling new or more products to rent-to-own models and second-hand trading. These forward-looking practices are taking root in industries such as automobiles, retail and real estate.

Innovative Business in the Automobile Sector

A host of innovative businesses have emerged thanks to the "sharing mindset", collectively known as "producing a car that can be sold infinitely".

- Hourly-based car rental

Hourly-based car rental is similar to commercial car sharing. In 1948, the Zurich Cooperative launched the first car sharing program. Later on, a great many commercial car-sharing companies emerged in the 1990s. Starting in 2010, auto makers launched car-sharing businesses that deployed both traditional and electric vehicles.

With a similar model, hourly-based car-sharing businesses chiefly provide users with convenient on-demand rentals based on technologies such as GPS and "electronic keys": Registered users use GPS to find the nearest "sharing car" on smartphones and use electronic keys to access the vehicles. After using the car, users drive back to its original parking spot or park it in another "car-sharing location". In this way, a car can be reused by others, improving the usage efficiency of vehicles.

Globally, car maker giants in Germany, the United States, and France have promoted car sharing services as "strategic businesses".

Daimler Smart Transportation Services Group, a wholly-owned subsidiary of Daimler, launched car2go, an innovative urban green mobility program, in 2009. It was the first car maker to launch a car-sharing service, ultimately becoming the global leader in implementing this concept. By December 2015, car2go, with 1.1 million members, was successfully operating in 31 major cities in 9 countries across Europe and North America, making it the world's largest car sharing program.

In December 2015, car2go launched a car sharing project named "car2car" in Chongqing, which was its first "internal trial" in Asia. Its project is scheduled to become operational in 2016.

DriveNow, BMW's car sharing project, was launched in April 2011. At the close of 2015, it has operated in seven cities, including Berlin and London, with over 240,000 users, making it a car sharing project second only to car2go. Volkswagen, another German automobile giant, has also launched a car sharing project, known as Quicar, in Hanover in November 2011.

Car makers in France and the United States have not been outdone in the field of car sharing. In 2012, Renault Twizy launched self-service electric vehicle rental services. In 2015, Renault launched "Bluecar", an electric car dedicated to the car sharing sector in Europe, in the hopes of capturing the European car sharing market. At the CES Asia 2015 in Shanghai, Ford announced the launch of the GoDrive pilot project in London. The American GM has taken an interest in car sharing, launching a car sharing project named Maven in November 2015. Opel has launched a car sharing business called CarUnity in Germany.

In China, BAIC BJEV and Foxconn invested in founding an electric vehicle hourly-based car sharing company. In 2014, the company launched a service where users could rent full electric vehicles by the hour, known as "GreenGo", which incorporates business models such as B2C, B2B, and B2G (business to government). The B2G model has become a partner to the Chinese Ministry of Science and Technology, where it provides ministry employees with cars for private use, forming a precedent in the reform of vehicles for government use.

In both China and abroad, hourly-based car sharing rental services, represented by car2go, have brought about a new "car sharing" concept, replacing traditional business models in which fees are calculated on a daily basis and vehicles are rented and returned at rental outlets.

Car sharing offers the biggest advantage in relieving a slew of problems, such as road congestion and pollution caused by private cars in cities, while meeting the different travel needs of users. The University of California, Berkeley has carried out a survey on car sharing, which shows that a shared vehicle can meet demand equivalent to the use of 13 private cars. According to another survey, 15–25% of the members of car2go, a car sharing program in such countries as the US, Canada, and Germany, have abandoned the use of private cars.

Given the aforesaid benefits, many car companies are embracing hourly-based car rental as a strategic direction, which will exert a profound impact on urban traffic landscapes.

While some car makers have launched car sharing services and rent-to-own models in the sharing economy, other cautious car makers have adopted the middle-ground "sales + sharing" model for new vehicles. This strategy can be divided into two types, respectively sales and sharing.

Auto finance leasing, aka rent-to-own, is a popular way of purchasing cars in foreign countries. As car ownership and usage rights are separated, this allows users to use vehicles before actual purchase. Users acquire the right to use a car from the dealer through a long-term lease without the need to foot any down payments (apart from a required deposit) and pay rent on a monthly basis. Upon expiry of the lease, vehicle ownership is transferred to the user.

An analysis conducted by qianzhan.com shows that in developed European and American countries, the rent-to-own model is an important part of the auto finance business. It is also a highly popular method for marketing automobiles, given that it is convenient for customers. In the United States, cars sold through "finance lease" account for 35% of total sales volume. In Japan, more than 2 million are sold through leasing sales each year, accounting for some 15% of new car sales nationwide. Furthermore, this figure continues to grow. In Germany, cars sold in this way account for nearly 50% of the local automobile market. In China, however, the auto "finance lease" model is still in its infancy, with a far lower penetration rate compared to foreign countries.

In another model, car purchasers rent the idle time of vehicles purchased on a sharing platform designated by the car manufacturer. This reflects the mindset of P2P car rental.

Ford Motor released the Smart Mobility plan at the 2015 International CES, planning to carry out many pilot projects worldwide, including a model for P2P car sharing based on the sharing economy.

Ford Motor also works with America's Getaround and Britain's easyCar Club in its peer-to-peer car sharing project. Ford signs contracts with some consumers who purchase Ford vehicles on a car loan to rent their cars for short-term use by car borrowers, who then obtain income through car sharing to reduce repayment pressures. Of course, the car borrowers concerned must be qualified drivers.

Coincidentally, in 2016, BMW allowed customers to opt to rent out their cars on BMW's car sharing platform DriveNow when buying its MINI model. This service was first launched in the United States, and was later extended to other cities such as London.

Chinese enterprises have also pioneered similar services. In 2015, Yihai Mobility, a car rental company, in conjunction with Yidao Yongche, Tesla and other companies, launched "G-Car Club". Users of the club can own a brand-new Tesla vehicle by paying a membership fee of 100,000 yuan and a monthly usage fee. The car, when it is idle, can also be operated by the company as a ride-hailing vehicle, where the renters would earn a "sharing subsidy". Upon expiry of the agreement, users can choose whether to "buy out" the vehicle's ownership rights. This model is a combination of automobile lease financing coupled with P2P car rental services.

This new "buy + sharing" model benefits more car buyers through its flexible, diverse ways and low instalment costs. This will undoubtedly benefit to the development of the automobile sector as a whole.

In an era characterized by Uber and Airbnb, the automobile industry, along with society as a whole, are seeing fundamental changes. Car makers are keeping a keen eye the new market for car sharing, and taking actions to prevent being marginalized amidst these trends. "Producing a car for infinite sharing" is the new business paradigm that car makers are pursuing in the sharing economy.

Innovative House Rental

The *Guiding Opinions on Speeding up the Cultivation and Development of the Rental Housing Market* issued by the Ministry of Housing and Urban-Rural Development in mid-January 2015 aim to encourage and support the development of the rental housing market. The government is keeping an eye on the real estate market—behind the transition to a rent-to-own business model is undoubtedly an enormous pressure for China's real estate market to clear excess inventory.

According to data from the National Bureau of Statistics in December, by 2015, the floor space of commercial residential housing for sale in China reached 718.53 million m^2, a year-on-year increase of 15.6%. Based on a per capita residential space of 30 m^2 in China, the residential floor space for sale can accommodate over 23.9 million people, more than the total resident population of Beijing at the end of 2015.

As the sharing economy rises, long-term rental apartments, "makerspace", and short-term rental platforms provide an effective way for both the residential market and non-residential market to clear excess inventory. The idea behind is to bring into play the scattered idle resources through the sharing economy by relying on existing real estate markets, with a view to meeting the diversified needs of users and enterprises.

Real estate developers hold a natural advantage in terms of winning projects and improving operations. As a result, leading real estate developers take the rent-to-own approach when entering the long-term rental apartments or makerspace market.

- Long-term rental apartment market

According to research conducted by the Investment Real Estate Research Institute, the long-term rental apartment sector in China is in the early days of exponential development. The domestic rental market geared to the youth has grown to about 800 billion yuan. In the current era, many enterprises supplying high-quality apartments (such as Ziroom, YOU+, and Uoko) have emerged in the long-term rental apartment industry.

Given the potential market for long-term rental apartments, real estate developers including Vanke, K. WAH, Yango, and China Merchants have entered the long-term rental apartment market. Clearing real estate inventory through diversified operations models is also an effective way to liquidize assets.

VKY, Vanke's rental apartment brand, was launched in 2015. Guangzhou VKY Tianhe Software Park, the first VKY transformed from a village house, opened in February 2015. VKY Financial City Store, the fourth store in Guangzhou, opened in October of the same year. This is a long-term rental apartment converted from an industrial plant.

As described in the profile of VKY, "Your apartment will not be the end of your hard work, but rather the starting point of your dream."

VKY adopts an operation model similar to common long-term rental apartment platforms. The company leases entire apartment blocks or individual apartments from owners and then gives these apartments a standardized makeover. Then, these apartments are rented out to tenants under the Vanke brand, supported by community property management services.

Other real estate developers take different approaches. K. WAH designs some of its properties as serviced apartments which are rented out under the brand "Stanford Residences". Residential projects including those in Jing'an and Xuhui districts in Shanghai include some apartments designated for rental.

Yango adopts a model of cooperation with Yu Jian Apartment, a long-term rental apartment brand. Yango provides sources of housing while Yu Jian Apartment is responsible for overall operations and management of long-term rental apartments.

Whatever the methods, real estate developers which enter the long-term rental apartment market generally abandon the "one-off approach" where developers call it a day after selling the house that they have built. In addition to building and selling houses, real estate developers are exploring a path to sustainable profitability in the housing rental sector, which tallies with the idea of "use without possession" in the sharing economy.

- Entrepreneurial coworking

Makerspace is geared to the non-residential market. According to figures from the National Bureau of Statistics, of the total area of commodity housing for sale in 2015, the area of non-residential housing for sale among office buildings and commercial buildings reached 179.40 million m^2, accounting for 25% of the total floor space for sale. There is not only excess inventory in the residential market; the non-residential market also faces grim inventory pressures.

Other than clearing excess inventory through long-term rental apartments, there is another avenue open to real estate developers. That is the coworking model characterized by SOHO China.

In early 2015, given the "huge market space for scattered work and mobile work", SOHO China launched a mobile office product called SOHO 3Q. Defined as "coworking space in the mobile internet era", this project is an experiment by SOHO Group in the transition from "development – fragmented sales" to "development – ownership". It is currently operating in Beijing and Shanghai, and will be launched in second-tier cities.

A typical O2O model, SOHO 3Q project rents out the office buildings of SOHO China flexibly, with reservation, location selection, and payments processed online. According to plans by Pan Shiyi, "SOHO 3Q is neither an incubator nor an ordinary business center. Instead, it provides a place of exchange and platform for entrepreneurs, but office buildings remain at the core of its functions. 'Capital matchmaking' and incubation of startups should be left to professional institutions." This is wholly different from the positioning of Tencent Makerspace, which aims to build a full-factor business incubator.

Industrial properties and industrial parks developed from makerspace are comprehensive solutions for real estate developers seeking to build and utilize a market for idle real estate.

E-COOL, located in Shenzhen, with a total area of 45,000 m^2 and a floor area of some 100,000 m^2, is a "creative industrial park" built by China Merchants Property Development. Converted from "Sanyo Factory" in Shekou, it is one of the cultural industry bases in Shenzhen. With 6 independent buildings in the park, it is home to over 100 creative enterprises, which demonstrates the increasingly prominent effect of clustering creative and cultural enterprises.

Some municipal governments attach importance to the model of E-COOL, which may be replicated in more cities in the future to revitalize local industrial parks.

Economic restructuring is often accompanied by industrial upgrading. Given the great pressures created by China's economic downturn, the economy will maintain its new normal for the next five years. It is imperative to speed up economic transformation and upgrading. The real estate sector is being transformed in terms of scope and depth. Due to immense pressures from unsold and idle industrial housing and commercial housing, there is an urgent need to stimulate the market for real estate inventory and create value for these assets. In this context, the prevailing trends make it inevitable that real estate developers transform their business models and bring scattered idle housing into the market through such means as long-term rental apartments, coworking offices, and industrial parks.

Destocking and Innovation Can Exist Side by Side

Orsola de Castro, a British designer, notes that "Hyper production and the sheer availability of cheap clothing have made us forget the value of maintaining and repurposing clothes and textiles." According to statistics from the US Environmental Protection Agency, the US discards 26 billion pounds of clothes, textiles, and shoes every year. The quantity discarded by American consumers in 2009 increased by 40% compared to that in 1999, and is expected to increase yet another 40% by 2019.

As the internet industry develops in recent years, online second-hand goods trading has also developed gradually, which inevitably exerts an impact on traditional retail industries, especially the consumer durables and luxury goods sectors. However, there are two sides to such an impact. It does not necessary pose a threat to the market for new products, and may instead produce a synergistic effect.

IKEA, a traditional furniture supplier, launched an online sharing platform in Sweden in 2010, whereby IKEA members can sell second-hand IKEA products for free. On the surface, this platform does not bring any financial benefits to IKEA. However, this idea from the sharing economy contributes to customer loyalty, because the environmental benefits from the trading of second-hand IKEA goods is entirely in line with IKEA's business philosophy. At the same time, if consumers can easily sell second-hand IKEA products and receive cash, they have more money available to buy new IKEA products, along with more room in their homes to place them. By supporting the second-hand market, IKEA has successfully promoted a strategy to drive new sales.

Another representative retail company that supports online second-hand trading is American Patagonia. According to research by the University of Innsbruck published on MIT *Sloan Management Review*, Patagonia announced a collaboration with eBay in September 2011. This was perplexing news for the industry, as their collaboration would reduce garment sales. Indeed, the very idea seems absurd at first glance. Who would seek development by cutting consumer purchases?

Patagonia gave a cut-and-dried answer: The fewer customers buy, the more they share, and the less the environmental pressure caused by consumption. In order to carry out this idea, Patagonia and eBay cooperated in creating the "Common Threads Partnership", on which anyone can sell and buy second-hand Patagonia products. The most direct benefit it brought to the company is the brand effect. Customers mostly sell Patagonia clothing they no longer need, thereby increasing the circulation of their clothes, whether on the internet or in brick-and-mortar stores. Similar to the effect that IKEA achieved, this can indirectly drive the sales of new products.

The concept of second-hand sales is not a new one. However, Patagonia is unique because it convinces consumers on the grounds of buying fewer new products. Moreover, Patagonia also holds the view that it can benefit from such acts.

For retailers, the success stories of Patagonia and IKEA show that by supporting the sharing economy, they can lure environmentally-conscious customers, improve their corporate reputations, and tap new markets and consumers.

Encouraging consumers to make online second-hand transactions does not necessarily run counter to the purchase of new products. This is clear in the eyes of Chinese online retailers.

An increasing number of idle items have become the prevailing trend, as shown by the "Double 11" and "Double 12" online shopping festivals that have caused a sensation in the e-commerce market over the years. Consumer goods have become widely available, and consumption by the middle class is booming. Traditional trading of second-hand goods is beset with a host of problems such as fake goods, poor logistics and poor aftersales services. It is difficult to devise explicit trading rules and evaluation standards for commodities. As internet technologies progress, enterprises represented by Baidu, Alibaba, and Tencent, collectively known as China's BAT, improving the means of payment, credit systems, logistics mechanisms, and so on.

The existing traffic on platforms gives them the ability to attract potential users who wish to trade second-hand resources, thanks to their advantages in areas such as information on online shopping transactions and their ability to release information on second-hand products. Thanks to user stickiness, enterprises can shift from the comprehensive second-hand market to the field of second-hand transactions. In 2014, Alibaba launched Xianyu, an online trading community for second-hand products, mainly to meet the needs of buyers who want to resell products that were purchased impulsively. Users can log in using their Taobao account, and post information on idle items or other second-hand items purchased on Taobao. Transactions are completed in a "closed loop", including payment. In 2015, Xianyu was split off from Taobao to make its operations independent, which shows its importance to Alibaba.

Similarly, Zhuanzhuan shifts from information to transactions by relying on 58.com, an online platform for release of information on second-hand products. JD.com has also launched a second-hand trading platform called Paipai.

Apart from the Chinese online retail giants, Amazon, a foreign retail giant, thinks likewise.

According to TECH2IPO, the digital retailer Amazon has launched a patent that allows consumers to transfer digital files such as second-hand e-books, music, videos and applications, just as they would for second-hand books and TVs. According to the description of the patent, digital products owned by users will be stored in their personalized data storage space, namely the cloud. When a user transfers their digital file to another user, the system moves the said file to the personalized data storage space of the assignee and at the same time deletes the said file from the storage space of the transferor.

For retailers, a new way to embrace the sharing economy is to indirectly facilitate the market for new products through online second-hand product transactions, which produces a brand effect and extends the "use value" and "use time" of second-hand resources, a direction that undoubtedly embraces the concept of the sharing economy.

Second, Leveraging

If a company lacks the courage and resources of the abovementioned car makers, real estate developers or retailers to launch its own sharing business, it can leverage sharing economy concepts in carrying out business operations and raising funds through the private sector based on their existing businesses and operations model, such as crowdsourcing operations or equity crowdfunding. Many enterprises have already adopted this approach and met with great success.

Virtual Organization Model Under Crowdsourcing Is Born

Labor-intensive and knowledge-intensive enterprises can collaborate with crowdsourcing platforms. "Virtual employees" can meet temporary manpower needs, allowing enterprises to better structure their corporate labor force, and match the supply and demand during market peaks and troughs more flexibly, thereby responding to market demand more efficiently.

Labor-intensive enterprises process tasks through crowdsourcing on the market to save costs and also free up smarter full-time employees to concentrate on the areas that bring the most value to enterprises. For example, a pharmaceutical company, employees spend 20–40% of their time on supporting tasks (such as printing records, manipulating data, and scheduling meetings), and 60–80% on knowledge work. Pfizer now relies on crowdsourcing to fill these jobs.

Due to such changes in demand from corporate customers, more and more crowdsourcing platforms offer services in this sector. For example, CrowdSource, a third-party platform, chiefly helps customers (large and medium-sized enterprises) manage employees working in labor-intensive jobs. Any enterprise which requires large numbers of workers for labor-intensive jobs can meet this demand through CrowdSource. Launched in the summer of 2014, CrowdSource has upwards of 200 clients. What sets CrowdSource apart from traditional third-party agencies is that the company specializes in labor-intensive sectors, such as online retail and publishing.

Any company that requires workers at short-term notice can cooperate with Wonolo, a sharing economy platform that can meet urgent demand for workers. According to TECH2IPO, Wonolo is a recruitment platform for temporary staff founded by two entrepreneurs from San Francisco in 2013.

After job details are published, users who earn an income through the Wonolo app can accept the job and begin working within minutes or hours. Should an online retailer realize that it lacks enough staff to confirm orders, visit warehouses and locate merchandise that need to be packaged and delivered, the company can recruit workers on the same day after posting recruitment information on Wonolo.

Labor crowdsourcing is gradually becoming a prominent trend in China, mostly in the "lifestyle services" crowdsourcing sector. Enterprises can create a services ecosystem that allows public participation, mutual assistance, and mutual benefit, through a new sharing economy model that integrates diverse, idle societal resources. For example, Rongchang Laundry, a time-honored laundry chain, launched an internet-based laundry service Edaixi that recruits part-time workers from the community as crowdsourced "e-housekeepers." Users can place orders at any time on the Edaixi platform, and an "e-housekeeper" nearby would pick up the customer's clothes at a pre-arranged time and send them to nearby outsourced cleaners. This year, Edaixi has extended its crowdsourcing services from "e-housekeepers" to "e-meals", providing take-out services by enlisting the private kitchens of community residents. This marks the beginning of the company's quest towards an O2O strategy.

The outsourcing of simple and repetitive labor is only part of the crowdsourcing of services. An increasing number of professional jobs which are traditionally undertaken by full-time employees have gradually shifted from outsourcing companies to individuals in the crowdsourcing sector. Without being restricted by such factors as geography, industry or profession, this model where services are "crowdsourced" enables enterprises to make more optimal choices than under previous conditions of information asymmetry, especially in the creative services sector.

The "creative market" crowdsourcing platform by Procter & Gamble and the crowdsourcing model "creative e-commerce" by Quirky are notable examples.

GE and Local Motors set up FirstBuild, a crowdsourcing platform, for crowdsourced design and production. Outstanding designers, makers, engineers and students from all over the world are invited to help GE improve the design of home appliances. FirstBuild will adopt online co-creation on a global scale in conjunction with parallel offline "micro-factory" field manufacturing to more quickly bring new products to market.

ZBJ.com is representative of China's creative crowdsourcing service platforms. The platform offers eight categories of services: graphic design, web development, marketing, copywriting, video animations, industrial design, architectural design, and renovation design. Since its inception in 2006, over 5 million Chinese and foreign companies have crowdsourced services through the platform. The volume of transactions on ZBJ.com was 7.5 billion yuan in 2015, translating to an 80% market share.

In addition to companies providing creative services that canvass ideas from crowdsourcing platforms, platforms that offer knowledge crowdsourcing services are also emerging in other fields. In the consulting field, for example, representative companies include HourlyNerd and Eden McCallum. There is also Business Talent Group, a company located in Los Angeles that provides corporations with "interim executives".

Behind the "crowdsourced services" model is the disruption to traditional forms of business organization and operations by the sharing economy. On sharing platforms, corporate clients can operate in an "asset-light mode" rather than solely depending on limited numbers of regular employees. By integrating the world's potentially unlimited reserve of part-time/professional freelancers, just as Uber has brought together a huge number of private cars, corporations can more efficiently meet their business needs and more quickly tap the market, allowing them to innovatively restructure their operating models and achieve rapid development in the sharing economy.

Fanning the Flames of Entrepreneurship Through Crowdfunding

At present, entrepreneurship and innovation have become the trends of our times. According to the *Guiding Opinions of the General Office of the State Council on Developing Makerspaces and Promoting Widespread Innovation and Entrepreneurship*, issued in March 2015, online equity crowdfunding pilot schemes will be launched to allow crowdfunding to better serve widespread innovation and entrepreneurship. Without a doubt, this novel investment and financing model will have a profound effect on the Chinese economy.

For startups, equity crowdfunding brings together idle private capital, with far higher financing efficiency than traditional financing channels. In addition to funds, a company can gather consumer feedback on its products. Successful fund-raising for a project is equivalent to a mass advertisement. In future, financing activities by startups will trend towards multi-party, multi-dimensional benefits.

According to the *Ten Classic Cases of Crowdfunding in China*, 3W Coffee attracted "shareholder members" through crowdfunding. Through raising funds from the public, each "shareholder member" is issued with 10 shares worth 6,000 yuan each, equivalent to each person investing 60,000 yuan. 3W Coffee attracted a great many well-known investors, entrepreneurs, and senior corporate executives, including public figures such as Neil Shen (Shen Nanpeng), Xu Xiaoping, and Zeng Liqing. 3W Coffee ignited the fad for crowdfunding by Chinese café startups in 2012. Almost every Chinese city now has a crowdfunded 3W Coffee outlet. By taking advantage of "coffee entrepreneurship", 3W Coffee has extended its brand to such fields as business incubation.

As clearly pointed out in the *Guiding Opinions on Accelerating the Development of Support Platforms for Widespread Innovation and Entrepreneurship* issued by the State Council, the global sharing economy is growing at a fast clip, and internet-based innovation and entrepreneurship is booming. Novel platforms that support widespread entrepreneurship and innovation, such as crowd innovation, crowdsourcing, crowd support and crowdfunding platforms, have seen rapid development. New models and new forms of business continue to emerge one after another, while online and offline operations are increasingly integrated, exerting an extensive and profound impact on methods of production, lifestyles, and modes of governance that is characterized by a powerful driving force and enormous potential.

Enterprises can harness the crowdsourcing model to revitalize entrepreneurship, and leverage crowdfunding to expand channels of financing for entrepreneurship and innovation. This is without a doubt another effective way to embrace the sharing economy.

Third: Cooperation

Apart from their transformation and building a broader, community-based foundation for business operations, traditional enterprises can share business resources and clients with companies engaged in the sharing economy through collaborative business models, thus promoting their brands and reaping profits without the need to invest large amounts of capital.

OTA and Short-Term Rental Contract

Most research focuses on competition and collaboration between the industry for short-term rentals and the hotel industry. According to the latest research report issued by Morgan Stanley, hotel chains such as Hilton and Marriott International need not be unduly worried about the emergence of Airbnb, which has had a greater impact on online travel agents (OTAs). According to a survey of 4,000 tourists by Morgan Stanley, online travel companies such as Expedia and Priceline have suffered greater losses from the emergence of Airbnb.

One of the main services provided by OTA platforms is providing users with travel tips. However, when users opt for short-term rental platforms such as Airbnb, there is greater potential in tourist services arising from such scenario-based consumption, because landlords, as local residents, offer more targeted and authentic descriptions compared to commercial travel tips. Therefore, some short-term rental platforms have begun to offer services such as entrance tickets and car rentals. For example, as part of their efforts to develop one-stop travel paltforms, Belvendor and Muniao Short-term Rental are also providing services such as car rentals and entrance tickets, in addition to short-term accommodation.

This impact is only one aspect of the gradually converging business scenarios; there is also win-win synergy between OTAs and companies offering short-term rentals. For example, in 2015, qyer.com, China's largest one-stop platform for outbound travel, forged a strategic alliance with Airbnb, a leader in the sharing economy. Airbnb and qyer.com have linked their accommodation resources in 20 popular tourist destination cities around the world. Through Airbnb listings on qyer.com, users can visit the Airbnb website and make reservations. The collaboration between these two companies covers online and offline activities, joint marketing, and theme events in global tourist destinations.

Behind this collaboration is the complementary advantages of both parties. As an OTA website, qyer.com wields advantages such as information collection, data analysis, and demand analysis, while its sources of accommodation are far less than those of Airbnb, which has a wealth of featured houses. The alliance of the two makes possible the complementary advantages of online and offline resources for the complete O2O in tourism.

Integration of Hotels and Shared Workspaces

In traditional models of operations, the many telephone calls and confirmation procedures involved usually make it cumbersome to reserve a meeting room at a hotel. Meanwhile, like idle properties on Airbnb, hotel meeting rooms are gathering dust most of the time.

LiquidSpace has seized this market gap to help freelancers and other persons looking for office space to find workplaces that meet their needs, schedules and location preferences. While coffee chains such as Starbucks may provide more flexible workplaces for such people, an overly public environment is not conducive to giving full play to creativity.

To this end, LiquidSpace has established partnerships with Marriott, which provides LiquidSpace with idle meeting rooms to rent to entrepreneurs and owners of small and micro enterprises on an hourly basis, providing them with a greater range of venues for meetings or group discussions.

A similar case is the collaboration between Starwood Hotels and Desks Near Me, a platform focusing on shared workspaces. Such hotels, often located in downtown areas with convenient transportation, offer facilities suitable to the workplace requirements of both individuals and groups, along with internet access, video conferencing facilities, and so on, making it easier to meet the professional needs of workers opting for mobile workspaces. At the same time, the sharing model also improves the utilization of self-owned property.

Crowdsourced Logistics Gradually Becomes "Standard Equipment" for O2O Retail

Crowdsourced logistics addresses problems in traditional distribution, such as slow deliveries, high costs and inadequacies in door-to-door services through a broad crowdsourcing network founded upon location-based services (LBS). Physical retailers and e-commerce platforms are working with crowdsourced logistics platforms to bridge the "last mile" in logistics and distribution.

Whole Foods Market, an American organic food retailer, has launched partnerships with Instacart, a crowdsourcing company that operates a delivery and pick-up service, in 15 cities across the United States. After a user places an order at Instacart, crowdsourced procurement and delivery staff delivers their order within one hour. As a result, average customer purchase volume has risen 2.5-fold while weekly sales revenue has increased by USD 1.5 million.

In the "private kitchen" sector, deliveries were previously undertaken by the chefs themselves. However, large order volumes resulted in poor delivery services that sometimes affected customer experience. Hence, more "meal-sharing platforms" have opted for crowdsourced logistics, using nearby couriers to deliver orders, thus ensuring the quality of food and user experience.

E-commerce platforms are also progressively launching "open delivery platforms" to support their own delivery teams. These platforms mainly serve their own e-commerce businesses, such as Baidu Waimai, Meituan Crowdsourcing, ELEME Fengniao, and JD Crowdsourcing. Their existing order volumes have allowed these e-commerce crowdsourcing platforms to quickly dominate the market. ELEME Fengniao saw 500,000 orders per day one week after the launch of services while Meituan Waimai saw 100,000.

Logistics distribution is an important aspect of the O2O loop in the retail sector. Making deliveries more efficient and maximizing consumer convenience by working with crowdsourcing logistics platforms is also a form of business innovation under the sharing model

Cross-Sector Cooperation Between Giants Forms a New Ecosystem

Most industries active in the sharing economy are in their infancy or growth period, and the market landscape remains uncertain. By gaining a head start and having a say in the market, sharing economy platforms can construct a comprehensive ecosystem based on existing business logic and platform rules. A case in point is Uber, which has built an urban transport and logistics system that uses idle private cars to provide transport capacity.

In the Chinese mobility industry, ride-sharing harnesses "rigid demand + high frequency" application scenarios to become a gamechanger in the traditional mobility market and the second largest sector in the sharing economy after "shared finance". It also makes possible the emergence of phenomenal enterprises, chiefly represented by Didi, which accounted for over 80% of the market in 2015.

Didi, as a mobile transportation giant, is a one-stop travel platform that offers ride-hailing services, carpooling, designated drivers (***daijia***[1]), coaches, and test drives. Many partners from other sectors have joined Didi in jointly setting up diversified scenarios for ridesharing. Together, they have built an ecosystem featuring 3 models: cross-sector marketing, cross-sector operations and cross-sector platforms.

For example, Didi has worked with real estate platforms such as Leju and milike.com to introduce "hail a ride to view a house" services; with Mafengwo to offer "Hutong cars" that pick up passengers and also provides photos of China's iconic *hutong* (traditional alleyways); with AliHealth and Mingyi Zhudao to offer "summon a physician in one-click" services; with China Merchants Bank in auto financing to provide Didi drivers with instalment plans for vehicle purchases. Didi has also become a shareholder of ELEME, worked with restaurants to offer "order crayfish with one click" services, and with Helijia to stage the "Halloween Vehicle" event.

Didi has also launched an open platform with more than 300 applications to date. Another example is Didi's strategic cooperation with the Huazhu Hotels Group to add "private car" services to the hotel's App.

Cross-sector cooperation is found not only among mobility giants, but also common in other areas of the sharing economy.

According to research by the University of Innsbruck published on *MIT Sloan Management Review*, PepsiCo has worked with TaskRabbit, an online mobile marketplace, to promote its new soft drink Pepsi Next and attract new customers. In "Extra Time", a contest sponsored by Pepsi, winners will enjoy an hour of free services from TaskRabbit. Each round lasts 4 weeks, with 50 tasks assigned every week. It is noteworthy that multinational enterprises like Pepsi have built partnerships with the startup TaskRabbit. The reason for these partnerships is that PepsiNext's target customers are "young, ambitious and especially fond of technology". TaskRabbit's customers also include young and ambitious technology lovers. Through the partnership, PepsiCo can combine its brand with the "relaxing" services provided by TaskRabbit, allowing

[1] See trans. note in previous chapters.

customers to leave trivial tasks in capable hands and concentrate on full-time marketing scenarios in their daily jobs.

Cross-sector collaboration has become an international trend, taking on diverse forms and extending towards more fields. Diversified collaborations between traditional enterprises and sharing economy platforms allows them to complement each other's strengths, take advantage of hot topics and spark off discussion on new topics, to reap the dual benefits of brand promotion and market development.

Fourth: M&A

Traditional enterprises can quickly participate in the sharing economy market by acquiring or investing in sharing economy startups based on their strategic imperatives. Their product systems can be improved through the differentiated product services in the sharing economy. On the one hand, such practices can prevent direct competition with the sharing economy model, retain existing customers, and attract potential customers through the sharing economy. On the other hand, enterprises can rapidly implement business strategies through acquisition or investment and have a greater say in the sharing economy sector.

There are cases overseas of traditional enterprises acquiring sharing economy companies. A case in point is when Avis Budget, a car rental giant, acquired ZipCar, hailed as the world's first sharing economy company, in 2013 for USD 500 million to enter the sharing economy sector.

In 2016, GM acquired the technologies and assets of Sidecar, a San Francisco-based carsharing company, after investing $500 million in the ride-hailing app Lyft. According to cheyun.com, Sidecar was actually the first company in the world to propose the concept of P2P carsharing and had launched ride-hailing functions as early as 2012, when Uber and Lyft had not yet arrived on the scene.

GM has demonstrated its strategies and ambition in the field of carsharing by acquiring Sidecar, investing in Lyft, and launching the car-sharing project Maven.

In addition to the no-expenses-spared acquisition of sharing economy enterprises by companies such as GM and Avis Budget, traditional enterprises can also grow with sharing economy platforms and share the dividends of the sharing economy through shareholdings and investments.

BMW invested in the "shared-parking" startup JustPark, which is now a global leader in its field, with over 500,000 users. BMW has integrated JustPark's mobile app into its new MINI vehicles to make it easy for car owners to find parking spaces and make payment. GM is also a controlling shareholder of RelayRides, which is a P2P carsharing company offering short-term rental services.

In addition to the shared mobility sector, the hotel industry, fearing the loss of their customers to short-term rental apartments, have begun to carry out capital operations to join short-term rental platforms. Hyatt Hotels was involved in a round of financing by Onefinestay, the scaled-up version of Airbnb, which raised USD 40 million. Singapore's Ascott Group has become a shareholder of Tujia.com and announced a new joint venture for apartment management.

Investments by hotel brands such as Hyatt in the short-term rental sector shows that the short-term rental business is a potentially new business area for top hotel brands. Sean Hennessey, CEO of Lodging Advisors LLC, a New York-based hotel consulting company, has said that "it's only a matter of time before hotel brands start to cooperate with short-term rental companies, and other hotels may follow suit".

In the field of shared health care, the industry leader Mingyi Zhudao announced that the company has completed a 60-million-yuan Series A financing round led by Fosun Pharma, followed by Gaorong Capital and ZhenFund. This is an important move by Fosun Pharma in the sharing economy sector.

Be it through investment holdings or M&A, these traditional companies have realized the substantial benefits that they stand to gain by participating in the sharing economy, especially from the huge public attention generated by a customer's participation in an exciting novel model.

Looking back, the sharing economy has reorganized dispersed private resources via the internet. A supplement from the incremental market ensures synchronized transparency of diffuse real-time data on supply and demand, allowing platforms to efficiently and soundly match supply and demand. Overall economic efficiency is enhanced by connecting different groups with different motives to form a vibrant trading market.

Traditional enterprises have long sought to achieve "economies of scale" by expanding their operations, whereas "scale can be more economical" in the sharing economy. The sharing platform mitigates problems arising from information asymmetry. The mobile internet allows users to more quickly locate nearby products or services via real-time geolocation functions, allowing supply and demand to be matched efficiently and conveniently. If everyone can offer services and create value, a huge number of individuals can be brought together to create the "long tail effect".

Whether it be the aforesaid transformation, leverage, partnerships, or capital operations, traditional enterprises can adopt either a radical or cautious approach, and embrace the sharing economy in all manner of ways. Traditional enterprises have risen to the challenges of a new era in a timely manner, and rapidly adapted to current and future business models, thereby generating new sources of revenue growth in business sectors that are continually expanding. This is the right way to embrace the sharing economy.

CHAPTER 15

New Economic Practice of Sharism

During the 2016 sessions of the Chinese People's Political Consultative Conference (CPPCC) and the National People's Congress (NPC), Ma Huateng (Pony Ma) made a bold prediction: the sharing economy will become a new driver of economic growth. With scientific and technological advances, productivity and private wealth will rise rapidly, causing economic surplus to become a new global problem. Economic surplus creates surplus economic resources, which manifest as idle inventory and idle production capacity at the enterprise level, and as idle capital, goods and "cognitive surplus" at the individual level. The sharing economy is an economic model that boosts economic benefits by bringing into play the economic surplus on a large scale.

How should the sharing economy come into play amidst novel economic trends of grassroots entrepreneurship and innovation?

Sharing of Industrial Ecological Resources

The entrepreneurial economy, which is a new economy built upon innovation, supports and ensures economic innovation through institutional structures, policies and strategies, thereby promoting the sustained innovation and development of SMEs. Back in the 1980s, Peter Drucker defined the entrepreneurial economy as a "new economy", calling it the "most important and promising event in modern economic and social history."

M. Huateng et al., *The Chinese Sharing Economy*,
https://doi.org/10.1007/978-981-33-6494-3_15

This conclusion is drawn from the study of entrepreneurial activities during the US economic recession during the 1970s. The 1973 to 1975 global economic crisis led the US government to abandon the gold standard, marking an end to the dominance of the dollar, while the US economy contracted for two consecutive years. However, Drucker discovered an interesting phenomenon. From 1970 to 1980, the majority of the over 20 million new jobs were created by small and new enterprises. Despite the sluggish economy, the entrepreneurial economy managed to buck the trend and become increasingly active.

This trend was completely opposite to that after World War II. In the two decades from 1950 to 1970, three out of four new jobs in the USA were created by large companies or governments. In each economic recession, job losses were concentrated in new businesses or small companies.

By the 1980s, the Reagan administration initiated "supply-side economic reforms". This era was also a period of entrepreneurship and global expansion for the American IT industry. "Small" companies such as Microsoft, Apple, and Cisco were born during this period. As the American IT industry got off the ground and Reaganomics was implemented, stagflation in the American economy was abated and the US economy began to recover, with particularly strong performance in individual years.

The entrepreneurial economy has become a driving force behind China's economic growth. China is currently resolving macroeconomic problems through supply-side reforms. The entrepreneurial economy, driven by the "Internet Plus" government policy initiative, plays a prominent role in this era. China is in a stage of transition from investment-driven to innovation-driven development, with increasingly active entrepreneurship and innovation, and a growing entrepreneurial economy.

Makerspace plays an important role in the entrepreneurial economy.

The concept of "makerspace" was first proposed at a State Council executive meeting on January 28, 2015. Thereafter, state organs such as the Ministry of Science and Technology have issued documents promoting policies for the development and implementation of makerspace.

In the *Guiding Opinions of the General Office of the State Council on Developing Makerspaces and Promoting Widespread Innovation and Entrepreneurship*, it is pointed out that makerspace is a collective term for new comprehensive, low-cost, convenient, and open platforms offering entrepreneurship services that are built through market-oriented mechanisms, specialized services, and capitalization based on the characteristics and needs of innovation and entrepreneurship in the Internet era. Such platforms provide entrepreneurs with a place for work, internet access, social networking and resource sharing.

From the perspective of specific business models, makerspace serves startups, entrepreneurs, and the internal "entrepreneurial departments" of mature companies. Based on their own core and third-party resources, makerspaces bring together investors and media organizations through online and offline platforms to provide entrepreneurs with intensive, one-stop supporting services, as well as low-cost office environments, hardware, and software, allowing entrepreneurs to concentrate on their core businesses, such as product development and operations.

During the various stages of entrepreneurship, such as innovation, team building, financing and marketing, makerspaces provide corresponding services to help enterprises solve the various problems encountered during the growth stage.

How to Share Resources

At the 2014 Global Partner Conference, the Tencent Open Platform proposed the "Double Hundred Plan", namely "to support 100 startups with resources worth ten billion yuan." Relying on the core resources of the Tencent family of platforms, this plan provides resources to outstanding entrepreneurial teams and speeds up project growth, remaining ever-committed to becoming the top accelerator for Chinese entrepreneurship.

At the Tencent Global Partner Conference in 2015, Ren Yuxin, Chief Operating Officer at Tencent, said that the Tencent Open Platform has linked up with over 4 million applications over the past five years. As of April 2015, partner companies have reaped more than 10 billion yuan in revenue from the platform, equivalent to creating 50 billionaires. Over 20 companies are now publicly listed, either through their own merits or "reverse takeovers".

According to Hou Xiaonan, head of Tencent Makerspace, to help entrepreneurs resolve issues regarding fundraising, talent recruitment, employee training, and brand awareness, Tencent Makerspace has launched the sharing of resources with respect to "open funding, open teams, open classes and open voices".

In response to the financing needs of entrepreneurial teams, Tencent Makerspace officially launched a venture capital alliance service in 2015. This project, known as "OPEN FUND", provides entrepreneurs and investors with investment and financing "matchmaking" services through the venture capital alliance platform, such as "open funding training" and "Tencent Open Day". More than 40% of participating teams have received "intentions to participate in the next round of financing." In response to the different demand for financing from entrepreneurs at different stages, Tencent Makerspace brings together the industry's top angel investors and venture capital firms, linking the closed growth loop of "angel investment – incubation & growth – next round of financing", together with pre-investment counseling and structured, targeted "matchmaking".

In response to the common problems faced by entrepreneurial teams in recruitment, Tencent Makerspace launched "talent recruitment resource sharing". Known as "OPEN TEAM", this project aims to build a service platform that acquaints entrepreneurs and professionals, leveraging upon internal and external partners to create a "core talent pool". Held every two weeks, the project organizes offline sharing and matching services in each city where Tencent Makerspace has a presence. Tencent Makerspace builds a core talent pool in cooperation with the in-house "Tencent University", human resources and recruitment mangers, communities of former employees of Baidu, Alibaba and Tencent (BAT), recruitment websites, and headhunting, and invites the founders of high-quality projects for personal interaction and recruitment, so as to meet entrepreneurs' demand for different professionals. At the same time, Tencent Makerspace, in cooperation with well-known talent agencies, provides entrepreneurs with talent recruitment services at different levels, including Nanjiquan and zhaopin.com.

The sharing of entrepreneurship training resources is chiefly to provide entrepreneurs with comprehensive training to enhance their knowledge and competence, including entrepreneurship knowledge and professional skills. Known as "OPEN CLASS", this project is geared to helping early entrepreneurs gain professional competence through short-term (each program lasts 2–3 days) training on professional skills such as product, technology, operation, and marketing. The Tencent expert group is formed in cooperation with Tencent University, Tencent Appstore, Tencent Social Ads, Tencent Cloud, Tencent Map, to share

Tencent's brand of professional skills such as product philosophies, technology, operations, and marketing, and meet entrepreneurs' needs for further improvement by bringing in well-known industry entrepreneurship training institutions or individual trainers to form trainer/training alliances. At the same time, Makerspace also cooperates with well-known industry institutions to provide targeted entrepreneurial training for entrepreneurs, including the Cheung Kong Graduate School of Business, Nanjiquan, and youmi.cn. Moreover, we have also launched the "OPEN CLUB" project through the "Open Class", providing intensive entrepreneurship camp services (the program lasts 3–6 months, with each round lasting 2–3 days) for company founders after high-growth series a financing.

The sharing of marketing communication resources focuses on providing brand exposure and public relations and awareness services for entrepreneurs. This project, known as "OPEN VOICE", enables a brand to have their own voice—learning to market itself and build channel marketing. Marketing allows a brand to attract attention from the media, investors, and job seekers, as well as boost traffic. Media services include media exposure targeted at venture capital and promotion by marketing agencies. Venture capital media alliances include online media platforms such as TechWeb, TECH2IPO, lieyunwang.com, Chuangjie, and TechSir.Com; "smart hardware media platforms" such as leiphone.com and Leikeji; O2O media platforms such as iyiou.com; as well as audiovisual media platforms such as 3 min Video and Danjie Entrepreneurship, providing entrepreneurship projects with media interviews and coverage. Marketing agency alliances include Kaigan, QIDAO SHOW, Koudai Expert/jiasuhui.com, Entrepreneurship Forefront, and Xinzhi Bailve, providing startups with different product packages at different prices that include consulting services, copywriting, media buying, ad design, advertising, and non-traditional media engagement.

The makerspace model, which stimulates surplus resources and speeds up the entrepreneurial economy is eagerly welcomed by governments. The Tencent Makerspace Flagship Demonstration Base was officially opened on January 6, 2016. As the participants pressed the "Launch-Off Rubik's Cube", six entrepreneurial projects in Shanghai such as "Diyidan", "Yijianrugu" and "Independence Day", as the representatives of the first entrepreneurs to settle in the new entrepreneurial park, received their keys to the kingdom.

Located in the central part of Wujiaochang in Shanghai's Yangpu District, an industrial park cum "demonstration base" with a total area of nearly 50,000 square meters jointly funded by Tencent and the People's Government of Yangpu District, is expected to be completed in three phases by the end of 2016. According to plans by Tencent Makerspace, over the next three years, Makerspace will share the product philosophies and pragmatic entrepreneurship experience that Tencent has gained over the past 17 years with Shanghai entrepreneurs, in an effort to incubate 50–100 stellar enterprises, and drive the development of Shanghai's internet industry chain through the incubation of quality internet-based projects.

Reconstructing the Sharing Ecosystem

The sharing economy is a result of the innovative integration of "Internet Plus" and traditional industries. Thanks to advanced "Internet Plus" technologies, the sharing economy is able to more cheaply and efficiently match surplus economic resources across society, thus stimulating and giving new value to nearly infinite idle resources. In particular, the key to the sharing economy lies in efficient and low-cost connectivity. In addition to matching supply and demand on their own platforms, sharing economy enterprises such as Didi and Idachu have opted to use the WeChat enterprise account as their connection tool.

Didi

Given that it manages a huge number of drivers, the Didi platform needs to be able to meet every passenger's specific needs, which requires the capacity to gather timely feedback on different needs at different times.

Before switching to the WeChat enterprise account, Didi used QQ groups, e-mail, WeChat groups, and app for the feedback of information. However, the information flow was fragmented. While this was bearable in the early days of product development, a host of problems were exposed after the company grew in size.

Through the WeChat enterprise account, Didi has developed Didi Classroom to help drivers familiarize themselves with both the Didi Chuxing App and urban traffic routes. Other applications such as the "benefits zone" and customer service (by human staff) allow targeted communication between different groups of drivers. More than 40% of daily notifications are read, equivalent to providing a 24/7 point-to-point communication tool.

More and more drivers have become aware of the Didi WeChat enterprise account. After the internal information management system was integrated with the enterprise account, functions such as instant messaging, knowledge sharing, release of official documents, benefits, order management, training services, and customer service have been developed. In the coming days, a self-service query function will be added. The greater independence of the platform has also lowered transaction costs and increased efficiency.

- Idachu

Idachu specializes in offering door-to-door "home chef" services. Idachu also considered creating an app for chefs to manage communications. However, merely software maintenance and developer salaries would cost hundreds of thousands of yuan each year. Idachu finally opted for the WeChat enterprise account, as "the cost of operating an enterprise account is equivalent to 1/10 of the costs for an app".

Once chefs and users are connected through Idachu's WeChat enterprise account, the user can place an order. The Idachu system will automatically find a suitable chef (alternatively, the user may designated a preferred chef), and forward the order information to the chef. Services can be improved by analyzing data on orders and chef services. In addition, WeChat's navigation services allow chefs to easily reach the user's location. The IM function that comes with the enterprise account also supports multiple formats (images, voice, text), allowing for smooth communication among chefs, customer service staff and users. This has effectively improved service quality and user experience.

Like sharing economy companies, e-commerce companies such as Midea have built distribution platforms based on enterprise accounts to truly achieve "flattened channels" and overcome past problems of excessively high online and offline distribution channel costs.

On this distribution platform, dealers recruit and manage distributors using the WeChat enterprise account. Distributors provide consumers with one-to-one services with regards to product recommendation, enquiries, and transactions through the enterprise account. Through the enterprise account, distribution staff can create their own professional image, integrate the mobile app with brick-and-mortar stores, and carry out routine management, order queries, logistics management, as well as check their commissions.

Enterprise accounts have also the sales threshold for distribution staff to the maximum extent possible while greatly improving user experience through one-to-one services.

It can be seen that, as a mobile app that connects internal and external enterprise operations management, the WeChat enterprise account has seen rapid development since its official launch in September 2014. By the end of November 2015, there were 600,000 WeChat enterprise accounts, with a total of 10 million users, 2 million of whom are active daily. In November alone, 12 million messages were sent and received via the app.

According to the *Internet Plus Restructures Organization Ecosystem – WeChat Enterprise Account White Paper* by Tencent Research Institute, the WeChat enterprise account provides a single lightweight portal for mutually incompatible software platforms by restructuring enterprise IT systems. The enterprise account leverages WeChat's advantages in the social networking field to reconstruct interpersonal interactions in the workplace and connect enterprises' real and virtual relationships. These changes in mechanism are precisely the "micro organizational revolution" and "micromanagement innovation" for various organizations under the "Internet Plus" initiative. It is also precisely the reason that the WeChat enterprise account has excelled in the sharing economy.

The WeChat enterprise account is a lever by which WeChat corporate users take advantage of the content and "relation chain" resources in the greater WeChat ecosystem. Creating a mobile app platform that connects enterprises, employees, upstream and downstream players and IT systems to build an enterprise ecosystem in the "Internet Plus" era is key to systematically collating the complex scenarios of work-related social networking.

Compared to traditional enterprise software, the WeChat enterprise account offers interfaces with advanced functions and uses many third-party software applications to offer more choices for users. Secondly, it adapts to the trend of work-related social networking. Rather than being limited to the traditional enterprise-level IT market, it connects internal and external relation chains to help enterprises build their own mobile internet ecosystem.

As distinct from the service account and subscription account, the WeChat enterprise account is backed by real-world social relationships, thus having greater control and autonomy.

Tight Relationship Circles

For corporate users, the WeChat enterprise account is committed to facilitating internal communication within organizations and communication between organizations and related parties. As these communication needs are often underpinned by close real-world relationships, the enterprise account offers special settings that are different from the WeChat subscription account and service account. For example, companies can set separate scopes for connected users on their WeChat enterprise account. Based on this scope, enterprises can freely configure, with practically no restrictions, information content, direction of delivery, and the number of notifications based on different communication needs. The final result is that information is delivered in a targeted manner at a designated location at a designated time. This function is often used only in office scenarios.

Overall, a registered enterprise account has greater admin rights and interface support for applications. Through such configurations, the WeChat enterprise account helps enterprises and public institutions build close and well-structured "mini social circles" within WeChat's social networking ecosystem of WeChat. Within these tight-knit circles, there are employees, and also other relationships requiring close coordination, such as suppliers and customers.

Functional Ecosystem

WeChat enterprise account brings together the powerful functions of WeChat, such as payment, voice messages and video calls. These functions are enhanced in the enterprise account.

On the one hand, tight-knit social circles allow these functions to serve even more diverse roles. For example, users can make direct payments to the payee (enterprise) through the WeChat enterprise account. Because the enterprise account allows information to be sent to targeted users at a designated time and location, enterprises can issue WeChat "red packets", make transfers, and make payments to members through their account.

On the other hand, the WeChat enterprise account also makes its SDK (software development kit) available to third-party enterprise software developers. These developers can then integrate WeChat's functions, such as images and voice messages, into their own applications, allowing them to contribute towards practical and user-friendly office software ecosystems for the WeChat enterprise account.

It can be said that the WeChat enterprise account has created a dynamically evolving and competitive ecosystem. In the eyes of the user, the WeChat enterprise account is a tool shelf with unlimited space. Users have easy access to the tool shelf and software updates. On this foundation, the WeChat enterprise account platform has become a complete system of solutions.

An "Enterprise Account" that Serves More Than just Enterprises

The WeChat enterprise account does not just serve enterprises. All organizations that require close connectivity, such as schools, public institutions, and even associations without a business license, non-profit organizations, online communities, or a corporate division can apply for a WeChat enterprise account.

After an application is approved, the organization's members can find their colleagues' WeChat accounts and make WeChat phone calls even if they do not know their WeChat ID. An organization can also link its various IT systems through this portal for greater connectivity.

Connecting Organizational Ecosystems

Due to the strong stickiness and demand for work-related social interaction, the WeChat enterprise account has naturally become a mobile workplace hub and a core platform linking various parties, whether internally or externally.

In-depth integration of internal and external resources: WeChat enterprise account provides a lightweight single portal for office and social networking. This lightweight portal diverts the traffic for subsequent heavyweight office applications with complex functions.

Customized B-end software system: Inside the portal is an increasingly rich third-party development ecosystem offered by the WeChat enterprise account. Service providers that develop software centered on the WeChat enterprise account provide modular functional packages for enterprise account users, as well as development of software tailored to different user requirements. Users can purchase the office software packages most suited to them according to their different business models and requirements.

In the "Internet Plus" era, the ideal state of organizational management is to use the strong interconnectivity offered by the WeChat enterprise account (with regards to "tight relationships") to build a tight-knit social network with the enterprise as its own platform. Data is gathered through frequent interaction and exchanges among relevant parties. Upgrading and value creation are achieved through iterative analysis. In this way, each organization becomes a "platform-type", "ecosystem" organization and a big data company.

The Ecosystem Layout that Connects Everything

In 2015, Tencent announced its future development direction. Tencent will pursue only two things: becoming a "connector" and working on the "content sector".

All possibilities have their roots in connectivity. Tencent is committed to becoming a connector that links people with people, people with services, and people with devices through the WeChat and QQ platforms. Without being overly involved in business logic, Tencent strives to become the best connector for various traditional industries by heavily investing in the partners around the Tencent ecosystem.

In recent years, Tencent has also made plans regarding the sharing economy.

After more than a decade of development, Tencent has gradually grown into one of the largest integrated internet service providers in China. As a strategic investor, Tencent has also made investments targeted at "complementary advantages and forward-looking strategies". The sharing economy is a key aspect in fostering internet-based innovation. We stand ready to work with all investors in adapting to future development trends and ensuring the long-term development of the industry (Table 15.1).

Table 15.1 Sharing economy platforms

Sharing economy sectors	*Representative investors*	*Introduction*
Ridesharing	Didi Chuxing	A ridesharing giant and unicorn
	Lyft	Ranked second among ridesharing apps in the USA. Lyft has raised from than USD 1 billion in financing
Makespace sharing	Tencent Makerspace	A business owned by Tencent and the largest entrepreneurial platform in China
Shared finance	renrendai.com	One of the earliest P2P credit platforms in China, serving over 2,000 localities
Second-hand product trading	58 Zhuanzhuan	A market for idle second-hand goods under 58.com and Ganji, with more than 3 million registered users and daily turnover of 5.6 million yuan
	renrenche.com	A website for trading of second-hand cars, a "quasi-unicorn", and one of the Top Ten China Internet O2O Enterprises in 2014
	ttpai.cn	Online auction platform for second-hand cars, providing one-stop services for individual sellers, including on-site vehicle inspections, wireless auctions, and transaction paperwork
Crowdsourced logistics	Logistics QQ huochebang	Professional mobile app for logistics and distribution. "Logistics QQ" is geared towards cargo owners and "huochebang" is geared towards drivers

Sharing economy sectors	*Representative investors*	*Introduction*
	rrkd.cn	A business owned by Tencent that was established in 2013. Also the first crowdsourced logistics company in China
	G7 huoyunren	An online transport capacity procurement platform for cargo transportation and bulk logistics centered upon garages and personal contacts
Professional/personal services	Rongchang Edaixi	Quasi-unicorn providing O2O laundry services, including "e-housekeeper" door-to-door pickup and delivery service
Shared healthcare	WeDoctor	A unicorn that provides a platform for online medical services in China
	miaoshou.net	Mobile healthcare app offering doctor-patient communication, home delivery of medicine and "health dossier" management services
Shared Education	Crazy Teacher	Large-scale Chinese O2O extra-curricular tuition provider for primary and secondary school students. The company has completed Series B financing
"Self-Media"	WeChat	A business owned by Tencent that runs a free IM app with more than 600 million users, covering a host of businesses such as IM, mobile payments, public platforms, etc.
	Ximalaya FM	A well-known Chinese audio sharing platform adopting the UGC (User-generated content) model. It became the top Chinese audio sharing platform in mid-2014
	douyu.com	"Danmaku-type" live streaming sharing website, focusing on live streaming of games, as well as sports, variety shows, entertainment, etc. The company has completed Series B financing
	fm.qq.com	A business owned by Tencent that runs a trendy online radio app, providing online trials of musical novels, news, entertainment, gossip, etc.

PART V

Governance: An Invisible Driving Force

The sharing economy has managed to sweep the world because of an invisible driving force—government.

In response to the new wave of consumption brought about by the sharing economy, governments have unveiled various policies based on local realities. It is true that, on a global scale, there have been regional imbalances in the development of the sharing economy, and that the development of the sharing economy follows different rules in different countries. Nevertheless, judging by the goals of various policies introduced in the world's economies, we can discern a highly consistent purpose: foster the development of the sharing economy.

This can be said to be the "fundamentals" of the various policies regarding the sharing economy in today's world. Driven by the goal of promoting the development of the sharing economy, this provides the driving force for the sustainable development of the sharing economy at regional and national level through both differentiated and homogeneous policies. Current policies for the sharing economy focus on the development of the sharing economy, and the homogeneous and differentiated aspects of such policies.

How should the fundamentals be understood? We may approach this question from the following three levels: national strategies, specific stimulus measures and policy regulation.

First, a national strategy can directly reflect a country's stance towards the sharing economy. Often, strategies at macro level are intimately related to regional or national economic and political interests and highly correlated with development trends in related fields. An analysis of such strategies allows us to determine the state of development of the sharing economy in that particular region or country. Based on such analyses, most major countries have adopted a strategy of active response to the sharing economy.

Second, specific stimulus measures. Specific stimulus measures refer to the approaches adopted by a region and a country in response to specific issues. These measures are also a manifestation of differences and homogeneity. The analysis of specific stimulus measures gives us a better grasp of the specific approaches adopted by each region or country, demonstrates how policies differ across regions and countries, and provides a direct reference model for policymakers. At present, it can be seen that most countries adopt "five-pronged" measures in promoting the sharing economy.

Third, policy regulation. The emergence of new economic practices has always refocused attention on problems of regulation. All governments need to consider such issues as whether they should regulate the sharing economy, and if so, how such regulation should be carried out. Currently, government regulation can be characterized as "one body and two wings".

CHAPTER 16

China's Response

Policy Environment at the Macro Level

In China, the concept of a "sharing economy" was first proposed in the *Guiding Opinions on Accelerating the Development of Platforms to Support Widespread Innovation and Entrepreneurship* (GF [2015] No. 53) issued by the State Council on September 26, 2015. It is pointed out in the document that, given the rapid growth of the sharing economy worldwide, China must develop its sharing economy and cultivate new areas of economic growth, in order to seize development opportunities and amass new forces to drive economic and social development. At the same time, it would be necessary to promote novel "sharing economy service models" that integrate and utilize idle, dispersed private resources to stimulate entrepreneurship and innovation.

It was pointed out at the Fifth Plenary Session of the 18th CPC Central Committee on October 29, 2015 that China must stick to innovation-based development, implement the national cyber development strategy and the "Internet Plus" action plan, and develop the sharing economy. On the same day, the development of the sharing economy and the promotion of integrated internet and socioeconomic development were included in the *Proposal of the CPC Central Committee on Formulating the 13th Five-Year Plan for National Economic and Social Development*.

It was pointed out in the *Guiding Opinions on Speeding up the Cultivation and Formation of New Supply and New Impetus by Actively Giving Play to the Leading Role of New Forms of Consumption* (GF [2015] No.

M. Huateng et al., *The Chinese Sharing Economy*,
https://doi.org/10.1007/978-981-33-6494-3_16

66) issued by the State Council on November 19, 2015 that China needs to further develop its sharing economy, and improve institutional support for the development of new infrastructure such as new technology applications, personalized production methods, and smart microgrids; widespread expansion of the "Internet plus"; and the sharing economy models such as short-term lease of use rights, with a view to offering the institutional guarantees for the development of emerging fields.

On March 5, 2016, Premier Li Keqiang proposed in the *Government Work Report* that the development of the sharing economy will be an important policy in China during the 13th Five-Year Plan. During this period, China will move faster to develop new technologies, industries, and forms of business, boost the development of a sharing economy through institutional innovations, create sharing platforms, and develop emerging industrial clusters such as high-tech and modern service industries, thus creating strong growth engines. The report also states that the focus of the government's work in 2016 is to fully release the potential of entrepreneurship and innovation throughout society. The government will implement development strategies driven by innovation, promote the deep integration of technology and the economy, and boost the overall quality and competitiveness of the physical economy. To this end, China needs to bring into play the multiplier effect of widespread entrepreneurship and innovation, and the "Internet Plus" initiative. Platforms for crowd innovation, crowdsourcing, crowd support, and crowdfunding will be created. A new entrepreneurship and innovation mechanism will be set up, in which large enterprises and SMEs, universities, research institutes, and makers collaborate. China needs to support the sharing economy to improve the efficiency of resource utilization, while also increasing public participation and generating greater wealth for all involved.

The concept of "developing the sharing economy" was proposed in a document by the central leadership in 2015, while the 2016 *Government Work Report* proposed promoting and supporting the development of the sharing economy. The CPC Central Committee pointed out in 2015 that the development of the sharing economy is of great significance for cultivating new areas of economic growth in China, while the central leadership proposed in 2016 that the sharing economy will promote the implementation of the "Internet Plus" initiative and innovation-driven development strategies, as well as enhance the overall quality and competitiveness of the physical economy. These demonstrate that the development of the sharing economy has become a national development strategy.

Policy Measures by Local Governments

At present, several local governments have incorporated policies for promoting the sharing economy into their future work priorities, with a primary focus on creating an institutional environment conducive to the development of the sharing economy through regulations and supporting systems to enhance market access.

Encouraging Integrated Innovation with Regards to Market Access

Market access regulations for the development of the sharing economy chiefly involves the regulation of possible new market entities and the regulation of new forms of market transaction.

Judging by the various approaches and guiding policies adopted by local governments towards the development of the sharing economy, an important goal of developing the sharing economy is to promote the transformation and upgrading of traditional industries and harness entrepreneurship and innovation to cultivate new areas of economic growth. Therefore, when regulating market entities, it is necessary to tailor innovation to development needs based on existing market regulation frameworks. Specifically, quite a few local governments attach the same importance to the development of the sharing economy and the implementation of the "Internet Plus" initiative and have called for the expansion of new room for development by creating new capabilities and drivers of growth through the integration of the internet with socioeconomic development. This calls for speeding up the integration of cloud computing, big data, the Internet of Things, and the mobile internet with modern manufacturing, modern agriculture, and modern service sectors, spurring the healthy development of e-commerce, the industrial internet, and online finance, as well as the development of the sharing economy. Many local governments view the sharing economy model as new technology and new knowledge underpinned by the "internet mindset", and recognize its positive influence on promoting the transformation and upgrading of traditional industries, as well as on stimulating new economic and social potential. For example, the governments of Beijing and Nanjing call for promoting innovations such as internet-based industrial organizations and business models, along with facilitating the deep integration and development of new internet ideas, internet technologies, and internet models with economic and social fields, with a view to developing the sharing economy and stimulating new potential for economic growth.

On the other hand, a great many local governments have become aware that the sharing economy model may take the form of short-term leasing of the right to use resources. Therefore, they are likely to provide a relaxed regulatory environment with regards to new forms of market transactions and establish a corresponding market access system. The economic policies formulated by the provincial governments of Hebei and Anhui, as well as the municipal government of Dalian, have clearly pointed out that an important aspect of the sharing economy model is "short-term leasing of the right to use". The Gansu provincial government and Wuxi municipal government have pointed out that the key idea behind developing the sharing economy is to "integrate and utilize dispersed, idle private resources." It is also noteworthy that Wuxi municipal government defines the "sharing economy" in the *Outline of the Thirteenth Five-Year Plan for National Economic and Social Development in Wuxi City* to mean that different people or organizations share the means of production, products, distribution channels, as well as goods and services being traded or consumed. This reflects the "right to use" and idle private resources that may be leased, including tangible means of production and products, commodities, as well as intangible distribution channels or services. It may also include static means of production or products, as well as goods or services being traded or consumed.

Some local governments designate certain areas of the sharing economy for key or priority support, mainly in service sectors that can improve the people's wellbeing. For example, the Fujian Provincial Government proposes to offer new services in such fields as equipment leasing, transportation and mobility, tourism, housing rental, and "experience reviews", in order to develop new forms of business based on "Internet Plus". The Wuxi Municipal Government proposes to develop new areas of the sharing economy, with a focus on supporting the fields of express delivery and logistics, housekeeping services, education and training, media creativity, and rental services. In these industries, most goods or services traded (such as machinery and equipment, vehicles, houses, tourist services) are more or less regulated through a system of market access regulations. In order that these resources, which have been allocated through initial transactions, can be traded again, governments will have to make appropriate adjustments to existing market access systems.

Stimulating Growth by Upgrading Consumption Structures and Supporting Entrepreneurship and Innovation

The development of the sharing economy requires the mobilization of diverse, idle private resources. Accordingly, macroeconomic policies will be required to encourage the public to invest their private resources in new forms of production. At the same time, it will be necessary to encourage consumers to accept such new sources of product supply and product types, in order to form a healthy production and consumption cycle. To this end, local governments are encouraging widespread entrepreneurship and innovation and the upgrading of the consumption structure.

Specifically, in order to encourage the public to pool their knowledge for mutual benefit and share their idle resources to promote widespread entrepreneurship and innovation, the Gansu Provincial Government has proposed the promotion of the sharing economy model by marshaling the forces of the public to the greatest extent. In this model, scattered idle private resources would be integrated and utilized, e-commerce platforms oriented towards social services would be developed, while online and offline crowdsourcing of knowledge would be encourage, thus promoting a new model for pooling and sharing wisdom.

While encouraging consumers to embrace new models of consumption in the sharing economy and creating a virtuous cycle for the healthy development of the sharing economy, quite a few local governments have also promoted consumption upgrading and increasing mid-to-high-end consumption as two of the chief goals of the sharing economy. The main way through which this goal shall be achieved is to make use of the sharing economy, optimizes the production and supply structure, and efficiently matches supply and demand, so as to create a service ecosystem characterized by public participation and mutual benefit, and expand the consumption of online services.

Formulating Supporting Regulatory Systems

In terms of regulating market order, many local governments have defined their roles in the development of the sharing economy as providers of policies that support the growth of the sharing economy, and providing institutional safeguards for fostering innovation in industrial models, while exercising restraint when delineating the boundaries between government regulation and market mechanisms. For example, the Hebei Provincial Government requires subordinate agencies to adjust and improve systems that support the sharing economy models conducive to the use of new technologies, the development of customized modes of production, new infrastructure such as smart microgrids, the widespread expansion of the "Internet Plus" initiative, and short-term leasing of the right to use.

The Wuxi Municipal Government proposes to draw up sound rules, regulations and industry standards, build new credit-centered market regulation mechanisms, and create a more liberal policy environment. Efforts have been made to set up internet sharing platforms, improve network information security systems, and provide new growth impetus for the sharing economy. Industry standards and regulations have been formulated to regulate the development of the sharing economy, allowing the various market entities to better anticipate government policies and measures, and assist participants in the sharing economy in active investment and consumption. Moreover, the government has proposed improvements to network information security systems, demonstrating that the government has limited its role in regulating market order to the most important imperatives of safeguarding social order, such as protecting network communications security. This helps reduce market transaction costs and set up a credibility mechanism.

At the same time, Wuxi Municipal Government also proposes to construct new market regulation mechanisms centered upon a credit system. This shows that, while exercising restraint in the use of governmental power to regulate market order in the sharing economy market, the government is actively promoting the establishment of a market reputation mechanism, and attempting to use market discipline to regulate the order of the sharing market in a timely and effective manner.

Problems in Market Regulation

The central and local governments have promulgated many policies to support the development of the sharing economy and given greater latitude with respect to the substance and form of its development. Nevertheless, the actual development of the sharing economy faces obstacles in the form of applicable market regulation laws, which can be summarized as "one body and two wings": "one body" refers to the market access obstacles faced by the sharing economy; "two wings" refer to systems that support the protection of the rights of consumers and suppliers that are conducive to the development of the sharing economy.

Market Access

A reasonable market access system is a precondition for the prosperity and development of the sharing economy. However, existing market access frameworks are not conducive, in many specific respects, to the actual development of the sharing economy. This is because the sharing economy removes information asymmetry between consumers and suppliers on the market through platforms with a broad user base, allowing resources that have been withdrawn from the circulation channels after the first transaction or certain rights attached to such resources to again enter the economic cycle. The processes by which resources re-enter the economic cycle has an impact on traditional market access rules, especially in those industries or areas where franchising is implemented.

Take, for example, private cars. Prior to the advent of the sharing economy, private cars would only be used by individual owners or families. In the sharing economy, private cars that have been withdrawn from circulation can be rented by any individual through ridesharing platforms. This directly impacts the taxi industry, which implements franchising. On whether private cars are allowed to offer "ride-hailing services", there are two viewpoints. The positive view holds that market access regulations on ride-hailing services should comply with the principle of "whatever is not explicitly prohibited is legal" and respect the objective needs of technological and market development; private cars should be recognized as an effective form of resource allocation. The negative view holds that legally allowing private cars to ride-hailing services will lower the market access threshold for taxis and make the existing taxi franchising system ineffective. This may result in the risk of disorderly operations in the taxi industry.

These two different viewpoints reflect different regulatory attitudes and measures towards actual market access for ride-hailing services. On October 10, 2015, the Ministry of Transport issued the *Interim Measures for Administration of Online Ride-hailing Operations and Services* (draft), which was made open for public comment. The draft defines online ride-hailing services as similar in nature to "taxi passenger transport", and attempts to regulate these services based on market access regulations that apply to taxis, requiring operators of ride-hailing services to have a fixed place of business and register branches in the localities where their services are provided, as well as apply for administrative approvals from the relevant municipal or county-level road transport regulatory agency. On the other hand, before the promulgation of the *Interim Measures for Administration of Online Ride-hailing Operations and Services*, Shanghai, Yiwu, and other cities had already launched pilot scheme to legalize ride-hailing services: Shanghai issued the first domestic online car-hailing platform license to Didi and implemented trial regulations where "government manages platforms and platforms manage vehicles and drivers."

Consumer Protection

Creating a sound supporting system for the protection of consumer interests and rights can play a role in guaranteeing the safety of transactions during the development of the sharing economy. A sound credit reporting system in the internet era can safeguard the rights and interests of consumers in the sharing economy. This is because the sharing economy makes it possible for strangers to exchange resources. The trust of parties to the transaction in the other party's performance capabilities is the direct factor behind a successful transaction. Therefore, the credit system is a necessary precondition for the orderly development of the sharing economy. It is also the first line of defense for the protection of consumer rights in the sharing economy model. The sharing platform can establish a sound credit information system to safeguard consumers by reviewing the qualifications of parties to a transaction and "scoring" their contract performance.

However, the best credit reporting systems in China, including the financial credit system represented by the Credit Reference Center of the

People's Bank of China, commercial credit information, and administrative and regulatory credit information (including public security, industry and commerce, taxation, customs, etc.) are not shared with sharing platforms. Credit information is amassed by platform enterprises chiefly through their own operations, which undoubtedly does a disservice to sharing platforms that provide risk warnings before consumers enter into a transaction.

Protection of Practitioners

The sharing economy has given rise to many new forms of labor relations. The establishment of a supporting system for suppliers in the sharing economy can be a good impetus to the development of the sharing economy. Sharing platforms provide information on supply and demand, generating jobs for these service providers. At the same time, a mutual review mechanism for suppliers and users on the platform is conducive to employment equality, mobilizing labor enthusiasm and creativity. Therefore, more individual service providers have opted to set up businesses on their own, and harness their knowledge and skills to earn income by providing services through online platforms, thus becoming new self-employed workers. However, how to protect the rights and interests of these service providers deserves further discussion.

Policy Trends in the Global Sharing Economy

An analysis of the major policies on the sharing economy adopted by major countries allows us to make the following judgments about future policy trends:

First, more countries will treat the development of the sharing economy as a national strategy

The development of the sharing economy is mentioned in the Communiqué of the Fifth Plenary Session of the 18th CPC Central Committee. The sharing economy was written into the resolution of the Party's plenary, marking the formal inclusion of the sharing economy in the strategic plans of the Party and the state. Moreover, the EU, the US, Britain, France, Japan, and South Korea have also unveiled policies to support and encourage the development of the sharing economy as part of their national strategic planning. Jeremy Rifkin, author of *The Third*

Industrial Revolution, once made three predictions about the future world, one of which is "the collaborative sharing economy will turn the operating mode of many corporate giants in the world upside down." Therefore, it can be foreseen that more countries will unveil relevant policies and implement reforms that spur economic development by stimulating the sharing economy, as well as upgrade these policies to the level of national strategy.

Second, innovative approaches to regulation and adjustments to laws and regulations in response to the development of the sharing economy

The sharing economy has been extended from industries such as accommodation and mobility to a host of traditional industries. However, enterprises represented by Uber and Airbnb have met with obstacles in terms of market access, security, and so on during the course of global development. Uber was limited, banned, and even blacklisted many times due to problems relating to their platform, driver qualifications and licenses, as well as safety. Airbnb has sparked controversy in many American states over tax issues. The sharing economy has come into conflict with the system because, on the one hand, governments are using traditional approaches when regulating emerging phenomena. On the other hand, access thresholds, compliance requirements, labor protections, and so on imposed by laws and regulations have prevented the sharing economy from entering relevant industries and becoming bigger and stronger. Therefore, innovative approaches to regulation and adjustments to laws and regulations will be inevitable for countries seeking to promote and encourage the development of the sharing economy.

Third, from uniform regulation to collaborative governance

Judging by how different countries manage the sharing economy, a prevailing trend is the shift from uniform regulation to collaborative governance. While being similar on the surface, governance and regulation are entirely different concepts. Regulation stresses unilateral government management, whereas the sharing economy is rooted in online platforms, and places more emphasis on diversified participation, involving minimum levels of government management, along with self-discipline on the part of enterprises and industries, better consumer awareness, public participation, social regulation, and so on. Furthermore, compared to government regulation, the idea of governance places more emphasis on the power of the market. The goal of regulation can be achieved through full market competition. Therefore, it is obviously not advisable to apply regulations on traditional forms of business to the sharing economy. In the early days of the development of the sharing economy, a collaborative governance model is a necessary choice. On the one hand, it is necessary to maintain minimum safety and quality standards. On the other hand, it is necessary to make room for the innovative development of the sharing economy. Government regulation should intervene only in the event of market or "platform failure". There is no need for undue intervention and regulation when a platform can reasonably control risk through its own policies.

Fourth, there is an urgent need for rules and regulations on new forms of labor relations

It is common for sharing economy platforms to face issues regarding labor rights. For example, in June 2015, the California Labor Commissioner's Office affirmed that an Uber driver is an Uber employee, rather than an independent contract worker (which Uber has always maintained). Article 18 of the *Interim Measures for Administration of Online Ride-hailing Operations and Services* (draft for public comment) also stipulated that operators of ride-hailing services sign labor contracts with drivers. This policy has raised doubts and opposition in the industry. In fact, the relationship between a platform and consumers/suppliers is distinct from the traditional relationship between employers, employees, and consumers. Employers are required to sign labor contracts with employees and are accountable to consumers for their employees' performance. If the traditional labor relationship is applied to sharing economy platforms, sharing economy platforms will inevitably become traditional business organizations, resulting in the loss of the environment on which the sharing economy relies for survival. For example, some online ride-hailing companies have over 1 million drivers and will surely become the largest employers in the world if required to sign labor contracts with all drivers, whereas Amazon—the internet company with the largest number of employees—has merely 100,000 employees. The corresponding costs of compulsory labor security and benefits will result in huge operating costs, which is a hammer blow to a startup. Therefore, exploring and creating new forms of labor relations has become a top priority for governments seeking to promote the sharing economy.

Suggestions and Countermeasures

Based on future trends, how would China respond to this? After some research, we have come up with the following ideas:

First, shifting from "regulation" to "governance" at the macro policy level

For China to achieve the strong development of the sharing economy, it is necessary to adopt new approaches towards corresponding government management. The idea of "regulation" stresses unilateral government management, while the idea of "governance" stresses the power of the market. The goal of regulation can be achieved through full market competition. Regulatory authorities should take full account of the opinions of market participants. Open, scientific, and democratic legislation should be carried out. Authorities should place greater emphasis on market-based approaches, take an inclusive approach, and encourage and support the sharing economy, as well as view the significance of the sharing economy to China's development and transformation from a strategic perspective.

The development of industry sectors is promoted based on sector-specific policies and action plans, and a "negative list" system is provided for the sharing economy. In terms of the sharing economy and the "Internet Plus" initiative, the central government and local governments have unveiled a series of policy documents and action plans, but there are few policies that support and promote active areas of the sharing economy such as transport, food and accommodation, services and labor, retail, and finance. For example, in the mobility industry, which faces the most regulatory obstacles, a negative list for the sharing economy should be formulated by improving relevant policies, laws and regulations, and the "sensitive" areas of the sharing economy should be well-defined. Sharing economy enterprises in the industries outside the list should be allowed to operate freely, and the obstacles faced by platforms in terms of access permission and labor relations should be cleared.

Second, improving and implementing supporting mechanisms

The rapid, healthy development of the sharing economy is impossible without supporting policies.

First, efforts should be made to improve supporting systems, such as the credit reporting system and adopt flexible mechanisms such as public consultations and soft law governance to promote the development of the sharing economy. The sharing economy, which is based on trust, can reshape social trust. Credit is a "hard currency" in the sharing economy, and there must be mutual trust between consumers and service providers before sharing and transactions can be successful. Therefore, on the one hand, it is necessary to develop a credit reporting market, move faster to build the social credit reporting system, and promote the seamless integration of different credit reporting platforms to eliminate "information silos". It is necessary to promote the online disclosure and sharing of information such as credit records, risk warning, unlawful acts and dishonest conduct, and provide operators with services such as credit enquiry and online identity authentication.

Secondly, social security and benefits mechanisms need to be improved. Relevant institutions should provide necessary insurance and benefits for those participating in the sharing economy, and offer guidance with regards to employment in the sharing economy to help job-seekers gain experience and skills and earn more income. Sharing economy platforms are encouraged to cooperate with insurance companies to provide a compensation fund or to provide insurance plans.

The sharing economy can take root and thrive in China by tightening intellectual property protection, encouraging capital markets to offer financial support, and encouraging industries to form self-regulatory bodies.

Third, innovation in regulatory mechanisms and means at the regulation level

The idea of government regulation in China has gained widespread popularity. While being similar on the surface, governance and regulation are entirely different concepts. Regulation stresses unilateral government management, whereas the sharing economy is rooted in online platforms, and places more emphasis on diversified participation, a minimum level of government management, self-discipline on the part of enterprises and industries, better consumer awareness, public participation, and social regulation. Furthermore, compared to government regulation, the idea of governance places more emphasis on the power of the market. The goal of regulation can be achieved through full market competition.

Differentiated regulation and moderate regulation should be implemented. Differentiated regulation requires regulators to carry out analysis of specific issues. Given the nature of the parties to be regulated, and the difference between new "commercial species" and traditional ones in terms of business model, business practices, and so on, innovation should be encouraged in regulation, and trial and error should be allowed, rather than compelling a new phenomenon to comply with existing regulatory frameworks. The essence of moderate regulation is that regulatory authorities should be humble in the exercise of power. Regarding market innovation, the law of the market should play a greater role.

Security issues should be reasonably defined and resolved. As an emerging economic type and business model, the sharing economy faces security issues. However, it is meaningless to talk about security issues in a superficial manner. The right way to deal with this problem: First, whether business innovation in the sharing economy faces more security issues than traditional business models. Second, whether novel security issues can be resolved by supporting systems.

Fourth, empowering individuals through various ways

In the sharing economy, individuals take center stage, and the central status of the platform is merely superficial. The sharing economy can develop only when individuals perform well in terms of knowledge, skills, credit, and so on. Therefore, government needs to empower individuals through a variety of means. For starters, it is necessary to improve intellectual property systems, including for copyrights, trademarks, and patents, in order to safeguard the intellectual achievements of individuals in the sharing economy. Second, the sharing economy liberates individuals from the constraints of traditional business organizations such as companies. Finally, internet literacy must be popularized to remove the digital economic divide, so that all may benefit from the sharing economy.

Fifth, move faster to build the infrastructure required by the sharing economy

Further efforts should made to speed up the development of broadband infrastructure, expand internet speed and reduce the cost of internet access, to allow more people to join sharing economy platforms as service providers. "Sharing economy demonstration cities" should be promoted, where a city's existing public and private resources are integrated through a single sharing platform, thus efficiently matching supply and demand. The sharing economy should be incorporated into the scope of government procurement. By setting an example, governments will encourage all sorts of institutions to use sharing economy platforms to find suitable service solutions for areas such as travel and accommodation.

Postscript

This is the first book published by Tencent Research Institute on the sharing economy. Notwithstanding its shortcomings, the book reflects our thoughts on the possible forms of organization for economic activities in the information society.

As an antonym of sole possession, the act of sharing has been in existence since ancient times. Sharing is often viewed as the manifestation of human sociality and our altruistic nature and appears in the form of counterevidence of the rational man hypothesis in economics. In this sense, there is a distinct difference between the sharing economy and the act of sharing: The sharing economy is a voluntary market choice under the rational man hypothesis and has nothing to do with altruism.

By and large, sharing describes the separation of ownership and the right to use. In new institutional economics, Ronald H. Coase and Oliver Williamson regard the separation of the right to use and ownership as an important factor behind transaction costs. Specifically, since it is impossible to cover all possible changes in a contract entered into in advance, the nature of a rational man pursuing profits will inevitably lead to conflicts and disputes, becoming the breeding ground for moral hazard and significantly pushing up transaction costs. Stakeholders have to use means of acquisition to obtain property rights, namely residual rights to avoid confusion afterwards.

In this sense, ownership, which is an institutional arrangement, is naturally the most comprehensive and also most expensive means of protecting the right to use, and is the last resort in response to transaction

M. Huateng et al., *The Chinese Sharing Economy*,
https://doi.org/10.1007/978-981-33-6494-3

costs. As the Coase Theorem put it, if there are no transaction costs, all economic transactions would be completed on the arm's length market, and forms of production and organization based on capital, property rights, employment, hierarchy, and command would be abolished.

The absence of transaction costs has long been regarded as an ideal situation that does not exist in reality, just like the rational man hypothesis. It is for theoretical discussion only.

This did not change until the popularization of the mobile internet and the emergence of peer-to-peer sharing economy platforms.

In the technological revolution brought by the mobile internet, sharing economy platforms play the role of an independent trading market. Free and active individuals on the platforms become the basic units of specific economic activities. Due to advances in the quantity and quality of information, an independent evaluation system has been set up, trust and credit can be extended, and transaction costs are slashed. These point-to-point direct transactions may still fall far short of the ideal state of zero transaction costs, but the separation of the right to use and ownership has gained huge, practical economic significance for the first time in human history.

In view of this, it is easy to understand why we firmly believe that the sharing economy can generate tangible value, not merely "false prosperity created by venture capital", and "will not naturally die out after the end of subsidies."

We firmly believe that resources saved through sharing economy platforms will not disappear from the economic cycle. These economic savings, whether in the form of currency or physical objects, will be reinvested in economic activities through channels such as consumption, savings, and investment. In this sense, there is no reason to fear that the sharing economy is inhibiting new consumption.

We believe that long-term cumulative credit mechanisms and real-time feedback and monitoring of sharing platforms can eliminate conflicts and disputes that result from information asymmetry. Independent trading opportunities that were originally abandoned due to high moral hazards have become lucrative again, and traders who take a wait-and-see attitude to the market will return to the market. Online car-hailing and short-term rentals are convincing examples of this view. Whether in theory or based on the results of practical observation, sharing economy platforms can generate tangible economic increment.

We believe that a commonplace car parked in an ordinary garage is a consumer product that only incurs depreciation expenses, but it can also become an asset with a value that generates positive cash flow. An expense item is removed from the family's income statement and an additional asset item is added to the balance sheet. Numerous such families, if combined, can increase profits and assets, and decrease liabilities across society. This is not a simple thought experiment. It is already a routine fact thanks to the sharing economy.

For this book, we are grateful to Mr. Ma Huateng (Pony Ma) and Mr. Guo Kaitian for their recognition and promotion of sharing economy ideas.

Thanks are also due to Mr. Cheng Wei, the founder of Didi. As the eminent practitioner of the sharing economy in China, he shared with us his insights into the sharing economy in this book. At the same time, we would also like to thank emerging enterprises in the sharing economy sector involved in this survey, including tujia.com, Xiaozhu.com, ZBJ.COM, rrkd.cn, renrenche.com, and WeDoctor. It is their active exploration that promotes the practice of sharing economy ideas in more fields.

Thanks are also due to Tencent Research Institute's research and writing team on sharing economy: Zhang Xiaorong, Sun Yi, and Cai Xiongshan. They have maintained sustained and in-depth research on the sharing economy sectors and policies in the past year, and have yielded fruitful results. We express thanks to leaders including Brent Irvin, Xie Hu, Jiang Yang, and Cheng Wu, and colleagues including Shen Dan, Li Hang, and Yue Miao for their support for this subject. We thank colleagues at Tencent Research Institute who are involved in the writing and planning of this book, including Zhang Qinkun, Cheng Mingxia, Li Gang, Zhou Zhenghua, Liu Jinsong, and Cui Licheng. It is through collective collaboration that this book was published in such a short time.

Special thanks are due to the experts including Duan Yongchao, Jiang Qiping, and Zhang Xinhong for their support, especially Duan Yongchao who gave many opinions on this book. We thank many scholars and reporters involved in Tencent Research Institute seminar on the trends of the sharing economy, and friends from Onehome, Edaixi, etc. Your views and cases have provided strong support for our research.

I would also like to thank the many peers who participated in the collection and sorting of materials for this book and provided support for this research, including Jin Ning, Liu Jiaqi, Liu Yuling, Gao Yan, Hao

Pupu, Liu Tongyan, Zeng Wenwan, Zou Xunyu, Su Ya, Ren Shuitao, Hu Jia, Sun Na, Wang Shaotang, Li Siyu, and Cao Jianfeng.

We thank Mr. Lu Jun and Ms. Zhu Hong of CITIC Press and Mr. Zhao Hui, editor of this book, as well as Tencent Research Institute for establishing an efficient team.

Finally, I would like to thank the readers who follow the sharing economy and Tencent Research Institute. You are our biggest motivation. Your comments and suggestions on this book and the sharing economy will be greatly appreciated.

The trend of the sharing economy has ushered in a new era. Tencent Research Institute will continue to carry out research in the sharing economy and other new economic fields, publish the latest information and results, and serve as a connector between industry and academia. We look forward to working with colleagues involved in the study of internet social sciences in promoting the healthy and orderly development of the industry.

Si Xiao
April 16, 2016
Shenzhen Tencent Headquarters Building

The manufacturer's authorised representative in the EU is Springer Nature Customer Service Centre GmbH, Europaplatz 3, 69115 Heidelberg, Germany. If you have any concerns regarding our products, please contact ProductSafety@springernature.com

Printed and bound by CPI Group (UK) Ltd, Croydon, CR0 4YY
30/09/2026
02225323-0001